Ephesians

WHO WE ARE
IN CHRIST

Lifeway Press
Nashville, TN

ISBN: 978-1-0877-6326-2 • Item: 005837518

Subject Area: Bible Studies, Dewey Decimal Classification Number: 227.5
Subject Heading:Bible N.T. Ephesians—Study and Teaching/ Christian Life
Printed in the United States of America

Lifeway Christian Resources, One Lifeway Plaza, Nashville, TN 37234

We believe that the Bible has God for its author; salvation for its end; and truth, without any mixture of error, for its matter and that all Scripture is totally true and trustworthy. To review Lifeway's doctrinal guidelines, please visit www.lifeway.com/doctrinalguideline.

CONTENTS

EPHESIANS

A few years ago, some friends and I had the privilege of visiting the ancient city of Ephesus (in modern day southwestern Turkey) with a local pastor friend serving as our driver and tour guide. We, like the other visitors, marveled at the remains and imagined what life in this city was once like. This port city was the fourth or fifth largest city in the world, sitting at the junction of four major roads in Asia Minor, and was known as the supreme metropolis of Asia. It was the center of worship of the fertility goddess Diana (or identified with the Greek goddess Artemis). Now, you can only see the remains of the (former) supreme metropolis of Asia.

Cities and civilizations pass away, but the gospel goes marching on. The city of Ephesus may not have survived, but the letter to the Ephesians has survived. And it is a letter filled with good news about our identity in Christ and what it means to live out that identity in faithfulness and in the local church.

Paul's letter to the saints in Ephesus contains only 155 verses. You can read it out loud in about twenty minutes. To paraphrase Klyne Snodgrass, "Pound for pound, Ephesians may well be the most influential document in history."[1] The message in this short letter is life-changing.

The Benefits of Studying Ephesians

What makes this little epistle so powerful? Let me mention four points.[2]

First, Ephesians deepens our understanding of the gospel. Whether you are exploring Christianity, are a new believer, or have been a Christian for years, Ephesians is worthy of your careful consideration, because there is nothing more central to the Christian faith and nothing more vital to growing in the faith than the good news of Jesus Christ. So, dive in and discover more of the "incalculable riches of Christ" (Eph. 3:8).

Second, Ephesians magnifies the importance of the church, as much as any other New Testament letter. Paul, under the inspiration of the Holy Spirit, says some remarkable things about the church that should elevate our concept of the church (See Eph. 1:22-23; 2:11-22; 3:10; 3:20-21; 4:1-16; 5:22-33). This letter shows us what a privilege it is to belong to the church and should inspire us to love and serve our local churches faithfully.

Third, Ephesians may also be the most easily transferrable letter in the New Testament. Ephesians is not the most situational of letters. It is what's often called a "circular letter," distributed and read by the churches in the Asia Minor region and, therefore, comes to us in a more general form than some of the other epistles. Paul does not name specific false teachers; he does not mention specific problems in the church at Ephesus; nor does he include his travel plans as he does in other letters. As a result, Ephesians resonates with contemporary Christians because it seems that Paul could have written the letter to my church and your church.

Finally, Ephesians offers some very practical answers to basic questions about the Christian life. In the first half of the letter, Paul drills down on important doctrinal matters (chapters 1–3), and in the second half of the letter (chapters 4–6), Paul deals more with moral, ethical, and church-focused matters. The first half of the letter speaks to who we are in Christ, and the second half to how we are to live in light of our new Christian identity.

The Author

Paul opens with these words: "Paul, an apostle of Christ Jesus by God's will" (Eph. 1:1a). While some argue against Pauline authorship, Paul himself says he is the author (1:1; 3:1). Further, until modern times, Pauline authorship was universally accepted.

Formerly, Paul was a persecutor of the church (Acts 9:1-2), but God transformed him by His grace, and made him His mighty apostle to the Gentiles (Acts 9:15; 1 Tim. 1:15). Paul's life reminds us that God can radically change anyone.

As "an apostle of Christ Jesus," Paul underlines the fact that his authority came from Jesus Christ. Indeed, we hear the words of Christ when we read Ephesians.

He became an apostle by "God's will." God had a plan for Paul, and it wasn't being an enemy of the church, but a leader in the church (cf. Gal. 1:14-16).

From where is Paul writing? Three times in this letter, Paul mentions imprisonment (3:1; 4:1; 6:20). He may have written this letter near the end of his two-year imprisonment in Rome, about the same time as Colossians and Philemon, approximately AD 62. A lot of the wording in Ephesians appears in Colossians, and it is a good idea to read Colossians as you study Ephesians.

The Recipients

Paul writes "to the faithful saints in Christ Jesus at Ephesus" (Eph. 1:1b). Being a **faithful** Christian in Ephesus and the surrounding regions would not have been easy. Paul experienced a fruitful ministry in Ephesus, but it came with a lot of hardship (cf. 1 Cor. 16:8-9). Paul stayed about three years in Ephesus, the longest stay in his missionary journeys—three months in synagogue, two years in the lecture hall, and "a while" longer (Acts 19:8,10,22). While he had many wonderful opportunities, he experienced a lot of tears and trials (Acts 20:18-19).

There was intense spiritual warfare in Ephesus. The city was known for different forms of paganism. The culture was steeped in materialism, sensuality, superstition, and perverted idolatrous practices. In Acts 19:11-20, we read of spiritual awakening in Ephesus. Many people became Christians, and this dramatic account culminates with the burning of books, which probably contained spells, incantations, and other cultish practices. Later in Acts 19 we read of how Paul's Ephesian ministry threatened the commerce of those who made silver models of the goddess Artemis (cf. Acts 19:23-41), which stirred up intense opposition from the locals.

Ephesus was also home to the Roman emperor cult. The worship of the emperor was a prominent feature of life at all levels in Asia at this time. Caesar Augustus was spoken of as the "Savior." On coins, statues, temples, and other items there was the gospel of Augustus, but the church was proclaiming the gospel of Jesus. In this context of spiritual warfare, Paul's words to the Ephesians includes words like "authorities," "power," and "spiritual forces," and he emphasizes Jesus's lordship over all.

In the middle of this city were the faithful "**saints**" (Eph. 1:1b). The word saint (1:15,18; 3:8,18; 4:12; 5:3; 6:18) has its roots in the Old Testament, which speaks of God choosing a people from among the nations to be His (Ex. 19:5-6). Christ has made us, as Christians, into a holy people (Eph. 5:26). Positionally, we are holy because we are united with Christ. Now we must live in a manner that is consistent with this position.

These saints included some Jewish believers in Ephesus before Paul's arrival (Acts 18:24-27), but later it seems that the churches were primarily Gentile. These Christians needed instruction and leadership, especially about unity among Jewish and Gentile believers.

The saints may have lived in Ephesus, but were spiritually located "**in Christ**" (Eph. 1:1b). They lived in union with Christ. Ephesians mentions union with Christ and being "in Christ" more than any other letter, about thirty-six times. In Paul's thirteen epistles this occurs some 164 times. This is the heart of Christianity: to be united to Jesus Christ. You are united to His death and His resurrection (2:5-7).

Our identity, therefore, is in Christ, not in our performance, our popularity, our productivity, or our prominence. One of the most common questions during the end of the twentieth century was "Who am I?" This question continues to be a dominant concern in today's society, and the book of Ephesians reminds us that we have an answer to this question. As Christians, we are in Christ Jesus!

The Greeting

Paul writes, "Grace to you and peace from God our Father and the Lord Jesus Christ" (Eph. 1:2). By saying "Grace" Paul is not saying "Hello," but is rather giving a "prayer wish" for grace to come to the Ephesians. The same is true for "peace"—Paul was praying for God to bring peace to his readers. This grace and peace comes from "God our Father and the Lord Jesus Christ." What a magnificent picture of the Father in this letter (see also 1:17; 4:6). There is also a majestic picture of the Lord Jesus as the cosmic King of all. Jesus fills the mind of Paul.

Interestingly, even though the church in Ephesus had an amazing history, with amazing leaders, the final mention in Revelation 2:1-7 about this great church is Jesus saying, "But I have this against you: You have abandoned the love you had at first" (Rev. 2:4). Though they were commended for several things, Jesus pointed out this problem of being the church of cold orthodoxy. As we explore many doctrinal points in Ephesians, may the Lord use it to keep us from this problem, and instead use this study to increase our love for the Lord Jesus.

---

1. Klyne Snodgrass, *Ephesians*. The NIV Application Commentary (Grand Rapids: Zondervan, 1996), 17.
2. For a more thorough treatment of the letter to the Ephesians see my commentary, Tony Merida, *Exalting Jesus in Ephesians*. Christ-Centered Exposition (Nashville: B&H, 2014). Excerpts of this commentary are found in this study guide.

WE ARE CHOSEN BY GOD

EPHESIANS 1:3-14

Perhaps you have had a friend or relative that can talk on and on about a particular subject. All you need to do is throw out their favorite topic (e.g., sportscars, NBA basketball, restaurants, great cities, or music) and off they go! They hardly stop to breathe as they give you the facts about corvettes, Lebron James, Thai food, Paris, the best 80s bands, or whatever their thing is.

It is kind of like that with the apostle Paul in various places in the New Testament, only his subject is with the Triune God. We have such a passage here. In Greek, this text (Eph. 1:3-14) is one long, complex, and glorious sentence that oozes with God-centered worship. One writer quipped that this is the "most monstrous sentence conglomeration that I have ever found in the Greek language."[1] Paul begins blessing God (1:3) and just keeps the praise party going for the rest of the passage!

Made for Praise

This passage is so important because we were made for praise. Humanity has never had a problem with the act of praise; we have had a problem with the object of our praise. In Ephesus, the people had numerous objects of worship, from Diana to the emperor. The question then (and today) is not, "Do I worship?" The question is, "Who do I worship?"

A High-Level View

Unfortunately, this passage has generated a lot of debate because it around controversial topics like election and predestination (Eph. 1:4-5). While it is fine and good to have this discussion, we can miss the spirit of this text if our first instinct is to argue our position with another. The spirit of the text is one of worship. This passage should promote adoration before it sparks argumentation; it is about doxology, not debate.

The note of **praise** is struck in verse 3, and the sentence ends in verse 14 with praise. These bookends help frame the whole passage and show us the emphasis in the text: praise God.

Why worship God? Paul says, because God "has blessed us with every spiritual blessing in the heavens in Christ" (1:3b). The phrase "every spiritual blessing" shows the glorious scope of God's blessing to His people. In the following verses Paul mentions specific blessing after blessing. The phrase "**in Christ**" will be emphasized throughout the passage, as we cannot enjoy these blessings apart from our union with Christ. The phrase "in Christ" appears eleven times in these verses.

Observe also the **Trinitarian** nature of the passage. The opening verses are Trinitarian; Paul mentions God the Father and the Lord Jesus Christ and speaks of "every spiritual blessing" (alluding to the work of the Spirit). Further, though the structure should not be forced too woodenly, there is an emphasis on the work of the Father in verses 3-6, the work of the Son in verses 7-12, and then the work of the Spirit in verses 13-14. Paul is calling us to praise the Triune God from whom all blessings flow.

Paul also points out that our salvation is ultimately for **God's glory**. Look at the phrase "to the praise of his glorious grace" in verse 6 and the phrases "praise to his glory" (1:12) and "praise of his glory" (1:14). Why did God choose to bless us with this great salvation? That He may be glorified. God saves people for His glory.

The passage also highlights the **grace** of God in salvation. Paul speaks of God's "glorious grace" (1:6) and "the riches of His grace that he richly poured out on us" (1:7-8). Those who have received these riches should praise the giver of them.

Further, these verses highlight the **eternal scope** of salvation. This passage goes from "before the foundation of the world" (1:4) to the completion of the plan to "bring everything together in Christ" (1:10). It goes from eternity to eternity.

Paul speaks of being blessed "in the heavens"—a phrase only used in Ephesians. I think this gets at the **already/not yet** aspect of our salvation. Now we are linked with the heavenly realms because of our relationship with God. We have the benefits of salvation now, but we also anticipate the completion of them in the future.

Finally, note **who** should share in this praise: both **Jew and Gentile**. These spiritual blessings are for all who are in Christ. This passage is about praising the Trinitarian God! Our God is worthy of praise. Why should we praise Him? We have been chosen by the Father, redeemed by the Son, and assured by the Spirit.

Chosen by the Father
EPHESIANS 1:3-6

Paul says that God "chose us" (Eph. 1:4) and that He "predestined us" (1:5). These words scare some people, making them tense up, but they should not. These are Bible words. These words should inspire awe and worship.

The idea of God choosing (electing) a people to display His glory is not new. God chose to create the world for His glory. God chose Abraham to bring blessing to the nations (Gen. 12:1-3). God chose the nation of Israel that they might be a light to the nations (Deut. 7:6-8; 14:2; Isa. 42:6-8). Further, Jesus chose His twelve disciples to bear fruit and multiply (John 15:16). Paul adds that God chose what is "insignificant and despised in the world . . . so that no one can boast in his presence" (1 Cor. 1:28a,29). In Ephesians, as in other NT texts (cf. Rom. 9–11; Acts 13:48; Titus 1:1; 1 Pet. 1:1; 2 Pet. 1:10), we read that God chose individuals for salvation. These believers, both Jew and Gentile, make up the church.

The Baptist Faith and Message 2000 puts it like this:

> Election is the gracious purpose of God, according to which He regenerates, justifies, sanctifies, and glorifies sinners. It is consistent with the free agency of man, and comprehends all the means in connection with the end. It is the glorious display of God's sovereign goodness, and is infinitely wise, holy, and unchangeable. It excludes boasting and promotes humility.

This is a good summary as it preserves the tension of human responsibility and divine responsibility; it emphasizes the infinite wisdom of God; it highlights the humility this doctrine should create in us.

📖 EVERY SPIRITUAL BLESSING

Being in Christ means you have already been graced by God with a vast array of blessings. Paul refers to every spiritual blessing in Ephesians 1 and outlines some of the most significant for which we should be grateful.

Fill in the blanks to outline these blessings. What words would you add to the list?

C _ _ S _ _ N
P _ _ D _ _ _ _ _ _ _ D
F _ _ G _ _ _ N
K _ _ _ L _ _ G _
I _ H _ _ _ _ T _ _ C _
S _ _ _ _ D

[Answers: Chosen, predestined, forgiven, knowledge, inheritance, sealed]

Some argue that election here is primarily corporate rather than individual. God did choose a corporate body, but that corporate body is made up of individuals. In fact, the passage speaks about how individuals experience salvation. "Redemption," "forgiveness," "sealing," and "belief" are all individual experiences; so it is not an "either/or" but a "both/and." God chose a people for Himself, and that people is made up of believing, redeemed, forgiven members.

The Goal of Election: Holiness (1:4)

Paul says God chose us "to be holy and blameless in love before him" (Eph. 1:4). God's purpose is to bring us into conformity to Jesus (Rom. 8:29-30). In Christ our blame is removed, and His righteousness is given to us. God sees us holy as His Son is holy, if we are in Him. We have that status. This truth is mind-boggling! Now we have the responsibility of pursuing holiness practically—reflecting God's holiness and love in the way we live.

The Grace of Election: Adoption (1:5)

Paul's understanding of these doctrines is not mechanical and impersonal, but familial. God purposed to have a family for Himself. He purposed to adopt us as His children. What a privilege to know God as Father! In these few phrases Paul gives us a mini theology of adoption.

What does it mean to be adopted? It means to have all the rights and privileges that belong to the Father's children. It is also important to bear in mind that adoption has a horizontal aspect, not just a vertical aspect. Not only is God our Father, but we are also now brothers and sisters. The church is a family of adopted brothers and sisters.

The inspired apostle also tells us that our adoption comes "through Jesus Christ." It is only in Christ that we receive these blessings. He goes on to say that God has blessed us "in the Beloved One" (Eph. 1:6). We have been caught up in the love that the Father has for the Son.

And why did God adopt us? Paul says it happened "according to the good pleasure of his will" (1:5). We don't have all the answers to God's ways, but we know that it pleased Him to bring us into the family. He was delighted to adopt us. Verse 6 adds that God did it "to the praise of His glorious grace." Adoption magnifies the greatness of God the Father.

An implication of God's purpose of making us holy and making us His adopted children is that we have been chosen for a mission. God's children will take on the family business, carrying out God's mission. We will imitate God as beloved children (5:1). Being chosen by God is a privilege, but it also contains responsibility for making Christ known in word and deed. My wife and I have adopted five children, now ages 16-21. And our children will tell you that they enjoy the blessings of family, but that they also have chores to do! So it is with the church; we call God "Father," and know one another as "brother and sister," and each of us enjoy the grace of this identity, but also recognize the responsibilities that come with our identity as God's children.

Redeemed by the Son
EPHESIANS 1:7-10

We should also praise God for the work of the Son who redeemed us. Paul overflows with praise to God for His great redemption accomplished through Christ, the forgiveness that is ours because of His death, God's plan to sum all things up in Him, and the rich inheritance that is ours.

We Have Redemption (1:7-8)

Redemption denotes liberation from bondage or slavery. It reminds us of Israel's salvation from Egypt. Our redemption is spoken of as an event that has already taken place. Paul says, "We have redemption" (1:7).

Paul says that this redemption has come at a great sacrifice: "Through his blood" (1:7). Through Christ's atoning work, we have been liberated from the dominion of darkness (cf. Col. 1:13-14). John later writes that Jesus "loves us and has set us free from our sins by His blood" (Rev. 1:5; see also 1 Cor 6:20; Gal 3:13).

Forgiveness. Paul links redemption to the "forgiveness of our trespasses" (Eph. 1:7). It is only in Christ that we find forgiveness. If He has forgiven our sins, then we should pour out our hearts in adoration to Him. (See Luke 7:36-50.) The Psalmist put it well, "LORD, if you kept a record of our sins, who, O Lord, could ever survive? But you offer forgiveness" (Ps. 130:3-4 NLT). We would have no hope if Christ did not grant us forgiveness . . . but He has. Blessed be His name!

Grace. Paul attributes this act of redemption and forgiveness to the grace of Christ: "According to the riches of his grace that he richly poured out on us with all wisdom and understanding" (Eph. 1:7b-8a). Christians are the recipients of Christ's extravagant grace and kindness. We should never lose the wonder of His grace but fill our minds and hearts afresh everyday with the reminder of what God has done for us in Christ.

Wisdom and Insight. God's grace has also been displayed through the giving of "wisdom and understanding" (1:8a). This grace involves the wisdom to know how to live in light of His redemptive plan (as expressed in the following verses).

We Have Revelation (1:9-10)

Still in the spirit of awe and wonder, Paul says all things will be brought together in Christ. That is, history is going somewhere. History is not a treadmill going nowhere, it's moving toward a particular Christ-exalting goal.

Paul says that God has "made known to us the mystery of his will" (Eph. 1:9). In His grace, God has revealed His eternal plan to us—a plan that centers on Jesus.

What is this plan? It is to unite all things in Christ, things in heaven and things on earth (1:10). So in addition to the personal aspect of salvation, there is also a cosmic dimension to God's plan of salvation. Paradise was lost in Adam, but it will be restored in Christ when His glory is fully revealed in the future.

Assured by the Spirit
EPHESIANS 1:11-14

On top of all the other blessings already mentioned, Paul now mentions the believer's "**inheritance**" (Eph. 1:11,14; cf. 1 Pet. 1:3-4; Col. 1:12). The Holy Spirit is the guarantee, or "**down payment**" of our inheritance (Eph. 1:14). This too should lead us to praise.

Assured of Our Privileged Status

Again, Paul says that it is in Christ that we have this inheritance (Eph. 1:11). Apart from Jesus, our future is not hopeful; it's terrible. But because of Christ, we are God's possession, and through Christ we have received a glorious inheritance.

How has this happened? How do we have such a status and future? From a divine perspective, it is according to **God's sovereign will**: "Because we were predestined according to the plan of the one who works out everything in agreement with the purpose of his will" (1:11b).

From a human perspective, we have **believed**. Paul emphasizes the importance of personal belief twice: "So that we who had already *put our hope in Christ* might bring praise to his glory" (v. 12a; emphasis added), and "In him you also were sealed with the promised Holy Spirit when you heard the word of truth, the gospel of your salvation, and *when you believed*" (v. 13a; emphasis added). Once again, we see this mystery of sovereignty and responsibility. People receive salvation when they hear the gospel and believe in Christ.

I love how Paul calls the gospel "**the word of truth**." Coming to Jesus for salvation is a coming to the truth. Notice also, the movement from "we" (a reference to Jewish believers in vv. 11-12) to "you also" (a reference to Gentile readers in v. 13) and to "our" inheritance (a reference to both groups equally in v. 14). This anticipates the exposition of how God has reconciled us, Jew and Gentile, through the work of Christ (2:11-22).

What Paul has said in the previous verses is true for Jew and Gentile, but Paul is stressing a different point here in verses 12-13 with the pronoun shift. He is stressing God's sovereign plan in the ordering of salvation history. Paul is also saying that the Lord's inheritance is not limited to the Jewish believers. They obviously had a special privilege as the first to hope in Christ, but the Gentiles are also recipients of God's amazing grace.

In other words, there are no second-class citizens in the kingdom of God. All believers are God's possession, redeemed for His glory. Gentiles can be assured of their privileged status by the Spirit's work in their lives.

Notice, now, what Paul says about the Spirit's work. He teaches us about the sealing of the Spirit, and the guarantee of the Spirit.

The Sealing of the Spirit

A seal was a mark of ownership and authenticity. Scholars point out that it was used for cattle, even slaves who were branded by their masters. Owners guarded their property from theft by branding them. Those seals were external of course. Our seal is internal (cf. Eph 4:30). God puts His seal in our hearts.[2]

Paul refers to the Holy Spirit as "promised" probably because his new covenant presence was foretold (e.g., Ezek. 36:27 and Joel 2:28; Acts 2:33; John 14–16). What a privilege to live in the new covenant age and enjoy the assurance of the Spirit, and to be empowered for obedience.

The Guarantee of the Spirit

The Holy Spirit is the guarantee of our final inheritance. The Spirit is the first installment or the down payment provided for the glory that is to come.

Many times people compare the Spirit to an engagement ring, using this verse. However, an engagement ring is not part of the wedding. It is a promise, but it is not a down payment. A better analogy, as John Stott says, is the down payment on a house, which is the first installment of the purchase. So God is not just telling us about something in the future, He is bringing the future into the present so that we may taste what the future is like.

To the Praise of His Glory

Paul concludes this worship service, striking the familiar line: "to the praise of his glory" (1:14). In light of all that our Triune God has done for us, and in light of all that He has for us in the future, let us join Paul in giving God joyful and humble adoration for the great salvation we have received by grace through faith.

**The Library of Celsus in Ephesus was one
of the largest libraries in the ancient world.**

PRAISE HIM! PRAISE HIM!

Use the space below to write your own prayer of effusive praise for
what God has done for you. If you need inspiration to get started, try
using the words you identified in the **Every Spiritual Blessing** activity.
Challenge yourself to use them in one, long, run-on sentence.

Election

Perhaps some further observations regarding the doctrine of election may be helpful.

First, there is great **mystery** here. This passage addresses God's eternal, secret purposes (Eph. 1:4-5; 10-11). We do well to remember that "the hidden things belong to the Lord our God" (Deut. 29:29). We will never comprehend this mystery fully, and we should discuss it with each other charitably.

Second, while we want to affirm mystery, we should also **affirm the attributes God clearly stated in this text**: God is perfectly loving (Eph. 1:4-5), eternally sovereign (1:5), gloriously gracious (1:6-8), and infinitely wise (1:8). God's act of election is consistent with His character.

Third, even though the passage magnifies God's loving choice, it also shows the necessity of **personal belief** in the gospel. Look at verse 13: one must believe. Remember, this is one sentence. Election and faith belong in the same sentence, and it is a sentence that only God could write. Someone once asked Spurgeon how he reconciled God's sovereignty and man's responsibility, and he responded, "I don't have to reconcile friends!"

Fourth, our election is **in Christ**. We are chosen in the Chosen One. We were not chosen for anything good in us. God accepts us because He chose to put us in union with Christ.

Finally, in light of these things, election should **humble us** (cf. 1 Cor. 1:27-30). Election should never inflate anyone's pride. No one should be cocky when talking about God's grace.

PERSONAL REFLECTION

1. What does this passage have to say about worship? How does it move you to praise God?

2. Why should we reflect deeply on the doctrine of adoption? What practical benefit might a deep understanding of this doctrine have?

3. How would you explain to a non-Christian what Christ did to accomplish your redemption?

4. How does knowing that God works all things according to the council of His will affect you? Why is it important to reflect on this truth?

1. E. Norden, in O'Brien, *The Letter to the Ephesians*, Pillar New Testament Commentary. (Grand Rapids: Eerdmans, 1999), 90.
2. John R. W. Stott, *God's New Society: The Message of Ephesians,* The Bible Speaks Today. (Downers Grove, IL: InterVarsity Press, 1979), 49.
3. Stott, *Ephesians*, 49.

WE HAVE COMMUNION WITH GOD

EPHESIANS 1:15-23

What should occupy our prayers? How can we learn to pray? One of the most important encouragements to give someone wanting to learn how to pray is simply this: pray the Bible. Read, pray. Read, pray. This ensures that we are praying in alignment with God's will, and it will give rich variety to our prayers. As Pastor Tim Keller puts it: "Our prayers should arise out of the immersion of Scripture."[1]

Some passages in Scripture actually contain prayers, and these biblical prayers are really helpful in inspiring and shaping our prayer lives. We can read them, branch off various ideas, and pour out our hearts to God. Of course, the Lord's Prayer is one prayer that stands out as especially significant. But biblical prayers also exist throughout the Old Testament, and the book of Psalms has been called the "Prayer Book of the Church." Also helpful for developing a vibrant prayer life are the prayers in the epistles. D.A. Carson has a wonderful book of expositions on Paul's prayers, entitled *Praying with Paul*, which I have used in various settings, and from which I have personally benefited.[2]

The book of Ephesians contains two wonderful prayers (here and in Eph. 3:14-21), both are worthy of our memorization and prayerful application. This text (1:15-23) reveals some important truths about prayer, emphasizing prayer for knowledge and understanding. We need the Spirit's help to grasp the greatness of God, the supremacy of Christ, and the rich benefits of the gospel.

As we pray with Paul, we can observe three parts to this text: thanksgiving (1:15-16), intercession (1:17-19), and praise (1:20-23).

Thank God for Evidences of Grace in His People
EPHESIANS 1:15-16

In light of the opening section about God's grace in salvation (Eph. 1:3-14), Paul expresses his gratitude to God for the saints in Ephesus. He begins with a note of encouragement, reflecting on what he has heard about the Ephesian believers. Due to the amount of time that he had been away from Ephesus, and the probable circular nature of the letter, he does not seem to know all the Ephesian believers who will be reading it. Yet he is still praying for them.

Paul is thankful for two important characteristics of God's people: **faith** in the Lord Jesus and **love** for the saints. These are essential qualities of Christians. A Christian has faith in the Lord Jesus and has love toward the saints. These are basic Christian graces, with hope making up the holy triad, as mentioned in verses 12 and 18.

When Paul refers to his "prayers," he could be referring to the Jewish pattern of three prayer times per day (morning, noon, and evening). During these occasions, and any other times, Paul gave thanks to God for the Ephesians. If Paul had this in mind, then here is another good principle for prayer. A good prayer life is both ongoing and planned. In terms of ongoing prayer, we should "pray constantly" (1 Thess. 5:17). But we also need times to get away, like Jesus, who spent unhurried times with the Father.

So in verses 15-16, we see a thankful apostle. His gratitude to God for the saints is expressed in other places as well. For instance, to the troubled Corinthian church, Paul writes: "I always thank my God for you because of the grace of God given to you in Christ Jesus" (1 Cor. 1:4). Paul even thanked God for the cantankerous Corinthians! How? He looked for traces of grace and found that to be worth thanking God for.

Let me remind you of the need to recognize grace in others. It is easy to be critical of others. It takes a mature believer to recognize grace in others. Do you wear the glasses of grace or the glasses of self-righteousness or self-centeredness? Let us thank God in our prayers for evidences of grace in God's people—namely, faith and love—and let us also encourage the saints when we see traces of grace in their life.

Ask God for Divine Illumination
EPHESIANS 1:17-19

Now we get into Paul's petitions. He uses multiple phrases that get at the idea of **illumination**: "Spirit of wisdom and revelation" (Eph. 1:17) and "that the eyes of your heart may be enlightened" (1:18). Your heart has eyes! Paul is asking God to give the Ephesian believers spiritual eyes to see who God is and what God has done for them.

Illumination is the simple idea that God opens our eyes to know Him and His truth. Inspiration is what we refer to as the nature of Scripture. Illumination is how we understand Scripture. We need the Spirit's help in understanding His truth. God's mind is revealed in Scripture, but we need "Holy Spirit glasses" to understand it accurately and deeply.

God graciously opens the eyes of unbelievers' hearts at conversion, like Lydia (Acts 16:14). Here in Ephesians, Paul asks God to give Christians eyes to see who they are. The Psalmist prays something like this throughout Psalm 119: "Open my eyes so that I may contemplate wondrous things from your instruction. (v. 18); "Help me understand your instruction, and I will obey it and follow it with all my heart" (v. 34); "Make your face shine on your servant, and teach me your statutes" (v. 135).

The reason we often fail to seek the Spirit's illumination is that we have an inflated view of ourselves. We are tempted to feel self-sufficient, as if we do not need God's help. The first step to becoming a student of the Bible is having a heart of humility—a heart that says, "Father, please give me understanding." And a great thing to pray for fellow Christians is "Please Father, give him/her understanding."

Notice whom Paul is asking: "the glorious Father." The God of glory opens eyes to see Him! Our Father is perfectly capable of giving us all the resources we need. We are not praying to some little, weak God. We are praying to the only God, the "glorious Father." He is intimate, near, gracious to His people, and like a good father, but He is also glorious in His majesty, transcendence, and power. He who spoke the universe into existence can turn the lights on in hearts of people to see the glory of God in the face of Jesus (cf. 2 Cor. 4:6).

Why do we need divine illumination? Consider three reasons Paul mentions in this passage.

To Know God Better (1:17b)

Paul longs for the Ephesians to grow in their "knowledge of him [God]" (Eph. 1:17). This is a basic request, but one that should regularly be part of our prayers (cf. Col. 1:9-10). Many of our problems are symptomatic of this more serious problem. As Carson puts it, "The one thing we most urgently need is a deeper knowledge of God. We need to know God better."[3] Keller comments that it is remarkable that in all of Paul's prayers we do not find him appealing to God to change the believers' circumstances, even though they faced many challenges.[4] To be sure, it is not wrong to pray for God to intervene and change circumstances. But what occupied Paul's prayer was "what he believed was the most important thing God could give them…. to know him better" (Eph. 1:17).[5]

The beginning, middle, and end of the Christian life is about knowing God. Beginning: Jesus says, "This is eternal life: that they may know you, the only true God, and the one you have sent—Jesus Christ" (John 17:3). Middle: Paul writes, "My goal is to know Him and the power of His resurrection" (Phil 3:10). End: John writes, "We know that when He appears, we will be like Him because we will see Him as He is." (1 John 3:2b).

The beloved English preacher Charles Spurgeon of the nineteenth century put it well: "I go back to my home, many a time, mourning that I cannot preach my Master even as I myself know Him, and what I know of Him is very little compared with the matchlessness of His grace. Would that I knew more of Him, and that I could tell it out better!"[6] May we long to know Him better!

J. I. Packer, in his classic book, *Knowing God*, says that those who know God have four characteristics: great energy for God, great thoughts of God, great boldness for God, and great contentment in God.[7] He emphasizes how important this matter is saying, "Once you become aware that the main business you are here for is to know God, most of life's problems fall into place of their own accord."[8]

Let us pray for God to open our eyes that we may know Him better. Let us not be satisfied with simply going through religious motions; but let us pray for God to increase our knowledge of Him.

To Know the Blessings
of the Gospel Better (1:18-20a)

Knowing God better means we need to grasp certain truths about salvation better, and that's what Paul prays for next. He mentions three particular blessings of the gospel, distinguished by the word *what* in English:

📖 GOING DEEP IN PRAYER

Drawing inspiration from other prayers of the Bible how would you choose to deepen your prayers for others to focus on the spiritual? Consider the scenarios below:

A friend with a diagnosis of returning cancer

Unexplained job loss by a coworker

A couple who adopts a baby

A family member struggling with depression

A friend suffering a financial setback

Your son/daughter launching a business

A church member with a new ministry assignment

- "what is the hope of his calling" (Eph. 1:18a)
- "what is the wealth of his glorious inheritance in the saints" (1:18b)
- "what is the immeasurable greatness of his power toward us who believe" (1:19).

Notice, the third blessing just keeps going. I made verses 20-23 a separate point, but they are really a continuation of the blessing of God's power.

Hope (1:18a). Paul asks God to open their eyes to know the hope to which He called them. In eternity past, God called us. Then, by grace, we believed in the present. And our salvation also has a future dimension. We look forward to God summing up all things in Christ. Our salvation is marked by massive hope.

Paul prays that they may now grasp the hope of this calling. In Romans, Paul describes our hope as involving sharing in the glory of God (Rom. 5:2). He also speaks in other places of the hope of "salvation" (1 Thess. 5:8), "righteousness" (Gal. 5:5), resurrection of an incorruptible body (1 Cor. 15:19; 52-55), and "eternal life" (Titus 1:2; 3:7). This hope is rich and it is varied in the New Testament. To put it simply, God has called us to a distinct way of life with a glorious future hope. When we hold out the gospel to people, we are essentially holding out hope to people (cf. Col. 1:5). There is much suffering in this life; there are many dangers, toils, and snares, but glory is coming. May God open our eyes to know more of this hope and live in light of it.

Inheritance (1:18b). In the grammar of the letter this could mean the inheritance God receives (i.e., we are His inheritance) or the inheritance that we receive (cf. 1:11; Col 1:12). Since the text speaks of the wealth of His glorious inheritance, it seems best to go with the first understanding (cf. Eph. 1:11). Paul wants us to appreciate the value that God places on those who are in Christ. F.F. Bruce says, "That God should set such a high value on the community of sinners rescued from perdition and still bearing too many traces of their former state, might well seem incredible were it not made clear that he sees them in Christ, as from the beginning, he chose them in Christ".[9] In light of this, we should live for God's praise, and we should declare God's praise to the nations (cf. 1 Pet. 2:9-10).

Power (1:19-20a). This third request is the climactic request in the prayer. That is made evident by how Paul expands on power in the following verses (20-23) and by the incredible labels Paul applies to God's power: "immeasurable greatness," "power," "mighty working of his strength."

God's almighty power is available to His people. It is only by God's power that we will be able to engage in the spiritual battle described in Ephesians 6. It is only by God's power that we will arrive safely into God's heavenly kingdom, and His power is given to "us who believe" (v. 19).

Think about where some of the Ephesians came from. Some were formerly caught up in magic, the Artemis cult worship, astrology, and emperor worship. Their lives were dark (Eph. 4:17-19) until Christ saved them. Paul assures these new believers that God's power is supreme over all their enemies.

Dear Christian, the power of the risen Christ is ours to do battle against worry, temptation, doubt, and demonic warfare. Why do we often fail to rely on this mighty power? Added to the exalted view of self and diminished view of God is the failure to understand the spiritual battle we are in. The evil one and his hosts hate us, our faith, the church, our marriages, and our mission. That is why we must lean into Christ and pray for His resurrection power to strengthen and empower us to live for God's glory.

To illustrate God's mighty power, Paul goes to the resurrection. In the Old Testament they measured God's power by creation (cf. Isa. 40) or by the exodus, but now there is another, greater picture of power—the resurrection of Jesus Christ. This power is ours in Christ. Paul says to the Romans, "The Spirit of him who raised Jesus from the dead lives in you" (Rom. 8:11). This power is ours to witness, to overcome sin, to pursue holiness, to fight against the schemes of the devil, and to have great faith for mission.

Praise God for His Exaltation of Christ
EPHESIANS 1:20-23

As Paul continues in the spirit of awe and worship, he mentions four aspects of Christ's exaltation that should inspire praise.

Christ's Resurrection (1:20a)

God, with His infinite wisdom and power, has done what no man can do. He raised Jesus from the dead. Death is no little bug to squish; it is a bitter enemy that we will all face. Yet because of the resurrection of Jesus Christ, we do not have to fear death. Jesus has crushed it!

In his famous chapter on the resurrection in 1 Corinthians 15, Paul closes by saying, "Therefore, my dear brothers and sisters, be steadfast, immovable, always excelling in the Lord's work, because you know that your labor in the Lord is not in vain" (1 Cor. 15:58). Because of the resurrection, life has meaning. Our labor is not in vain. The resurrection changes everything. Praise God that the tomb is empty, and the throne is occupied!

Later in Ephesians, Paul gives more thought to the implications of the resurrection when he says that God as "made us alive with Christ" (Eph. 2:5). Christians are no longer dead in sin, for we have been united to the resurrected Christ!

Christ's Enthronement (1:20b)

Jesus is not only alive forevermore, but He is also reigning forevermore. Paul notes here the enthronement of Jesus.

In the early preaching in the book of Acts, the resurrection and Christ's enthronement was emphasized. This was the fulfillment of Messianic prophecies (cf. Ps. 110:1).

To be at the "right hand" was a position of privilege, honor, favor, victory, and power. This position belongs to Jesus Christ alone.

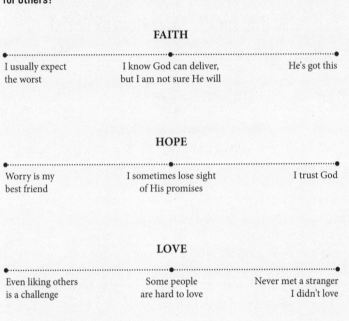

What does that mean for us? It means everything. Everything is under the reign of the seated King. The author of Hebrews says that He is upholding the universe by the word of His power, and He upholds it all sitting down (Heb. 1:3). If He is doing this, then we can trust Him with our problems—both great and small.

Christ's Supremacy (1:21-22a)

Christ as the risen King is now superior to every competitive power. His throne is above the principalities and powers. He is above creation. He is above Satan and his system. He is above everyone and every ruler. Paul mentions His supremacy over all earthly powers. He mentions Christ's supremacy over every title or name (cf. Phil. 2:6-11). And then he mentions Christ's supremacy over all His enemies with the phrase "under His feet."

Several years ago, my wife and I visited the Egyptian Museum in Cairo. One of the many striking things we saw was King Tut's throne and footstool. On the footstool were pictures of his enemies, illustrating his rule over them. While we enjoyed this amusing sight, it made me think of the King of Kings who alone reigns over all.

Christ's Headship (1:22b-23)

Finally, Paul mentions Christ's headship over the church. Here we see the amazing connection between Christ and His church. Only the church, not all creation, is said to be His body. Consequently, the church should be important to us. Jesus identifies Himself with it; He is head over it.

Paul says that Christ is "head over everything for the church, which is his body, the fullness of the one who fills all things in every way" (Eph. 1:22b-23). Jesus, as the head of the church, is filling His church with His Spirit, power, grace and gifts.[10] He not only reigns over the church but He empowers the church so that we may flourish and bring Him glory. Jesus rules and fills His church in a marvelous way.

What this means is that we are entirely dependent on Christ as a church. What makes us something significant—indeed glorious—is our relationship to Jesus. He fills the church with His presence.

What encouragement this must have given to the house churches in the region of Ephesus. What encouragement it should give to us, regardless of how big or small our church is, and regardless of where we meet together.

Let us thank God for evidences of grace in the lives of our brothers and sisters. Let us pray for God to open our eyes to know all that is ours because of the gospel. And let us praise God for the exaltation of His Son and our Savior, Jesus.

A CLOSER LOOK

Faith, Hope and Love

In a parallel passage, Paul gives thanks for the Colossians' faith, love, and hope, as well: "We always thank God, the Father of our Lord Jesus Christ, when we pray for you, for we have heard of your faith in Christ Jesus and of the love you have for all the saints because of the hope reserved for you in heaven" (Col. 1:3-5). The Colossians' experience in Christ—like the Ephesian believers— was marked by three glorious traits (see also: 1 Thess. 1:3; 5:8; 1 Cor. 13:13; Heb. 10:19-25).

Paul does not mention the things people today focus on, like the church's style, budget, attendance numbers, political influence, or other matters. He puts his finger on what is the real heartbeat of a church, what makes a church a truly vibrant church: faith, hope, and love. These traits come to us through the gospel, and they are the "family traits" of the church.

These traits should mark every believer, and we should give God thanks when we see these qualities in our brothers and sisters. It is easy to be self-absorbed or overly critical in the church, and miss these marvelous evidences of God's grace. These are not generic characteristics, but are Spirit-produced, Christ-centered, God-given traits. The gospel changes everything, for it creates faith in Christ, love toward the saints, and the hope of heaven. When we observe this holy triad in a fellow believer, let us give God thanks.

PERSONAL REFLECTION

1. What has this passage taught you about prayer? What is missing in your prayer life?

2. Why do we need divine illumination when reading Scripture?

3. What practical difference would it make if we understood our hope, inheritance, and power better?

4. What does this passage say about the exaltation of Jesus? How might living with this awareness affect your life?

1. Tim Keller, *Prayer* (New York: Penguin, 2014), 55.
2. D. A. Carson, *Praying with Paul.* Second Edition (Grand Rapids: Baker, 2014).
3. Ibid., xiii.
4. Keller, *Prayer*, 20.
5. Ibid.
6. Charles Spurgeon, "The Great Change." Sermon online at https://archive.spurgeon.org/misc/abio011.php. Accessed Aug 3, 2021.
7. J.I. Packer, *Knowing God* (Downers Grove: InterVarsity, 1973), 27–31.
8. Ibid., 34
9. F.F. Bruce, *The Epistle to the Colossians, to Philemon, and to the Ephesians.* The New International Commentary of the New Testament (Grand Rapids: Eerdmans, 1984), 270.
10. A.T. Lincoln, *Ephesians,* (Dalls: Word. 1990), 80. See also Peter T. O'brien, *The Letter to the Ephesians.* The Pillar New Testament Commentary (Grand Rapids: Eerdmans, 1999), 152.

WE ARE SAVED BY GRACE

EPHESIANS 2:1-10

P astor R. Kent Hughes tells the following (bizarre!) story:

> I have in my file a photograph of the corpse of the philoso-
> pher Jeremy Bentham, father of utilitarianism. The photo
> shows his body sitting in a chair, dressed and hatted in
> early nineteenth-century gentleman's wear. The whole
> thing is a result of his dark humor, for when he died he
> gave orders that his entire estate be given to the University
> College Hospital in London on the condition that his body
> be preserved and placed in attendance at all the hospi-
> tal's board meetings. This was duly carried out, and every
> year to this day Bentham is wheeled up to the board table
> and the chairman says, "Jeremy Bentham, present but not
> voting." This is, of course, a great joke on his utilitarianism.
> Jeremy Bentham will never raise his hand in response, he
> will never submit a motion—because he has been dead for
> nearly a hundred and sixty years.[1]

Present but not voting! Of course, he cannot vote because dead men do
not make decisions. And this is what Paul is talking about in this passage.
In Ephesians 2:1-10, we see how God raises the spiritually dead and makes
them alive with Christ. If you are in Christ, then a miracle has happened.
By God's amazing grace, He has given you spiritual life.

Allow me now to highlight three truths about God's work in bringing
the dead to life.

Apart from Christ, We Were Spiritually Dead
EPHESIANS 2:1-3

Notice our pre-Christian past. The picture is not good. Paul shows us who we were before Christ, with three descriptions.

We Were Dead (2:1)

Paul says that you were dead in "your trespasses and sins" (Eph. 2:1). This was our previous state of alienation from God. Paul repeats this later in this chapter in his amazement at what God has done: "Even though we were dead in trespasses" (2:5).

"Trespasses" draws attention to acts of sin. "Sins" is a more comprehensive account of the evil in humanity. We were wretched and culpable because of our trespasses and sins (cf. 4:18).

Of course, this is the complete opposite of what the world tells us about ourselves as humans. The world tells us that we are basically good, and if we just believe in ourselves, then we can do anything. While a spiritually dead person may indeed do amazing things because he or she is an image bearer of God—make works of art, play sports exceptionally well, make money, do humanitarian work—he or she can do nothing spiritually apart from Jesus (cf. John 15:5).

It is a sad predicament. We are not morally good. We are not neutral. To quote Miracle Max in *The Princess Bride*, we were not "mostly dead." We were totally dead. And we needed a miracle that only God could perform.

If God performed this miracle in your heart, then you should celebrate His grace!

We Were Disobedient (2:2-3a)

Paul goes on to describe how we disobeyed God like our first parents. Instead of following God, we followed three evil forces.

We followed the world. Paul refers to sins "in which you previously walked according to the ways of this world" (Eph. 2:2a). The unregenerate person is controlled by the world's influences and values, which are contrary to God's values. Consequently, we need Jesus to rescue us "from this present evil age" (Gal. 1:4).

We followed Satan. Paul goes on to describe another force at work, the evil one's influence: "According to the ruler of the power of the air, the spirit now working in the disobedient" (Eph. 2:2b). The letter to the Ephesians speaks more about demonic power than any other New Testament letter. And it draws attention to the power behind them: Satan (see 4:27; 6:11,16).

Such a concept seems archaic and ridiculous to many modern individuals, but God's Word could not be clearer about the reality of Satan and the destructive influence he possesses.

"Ruler" or "prince" in the Old Testament was a term used for a national, local, or tribal leader. In the Gospels, Satan is the "ruler of the demons" (Matt. 9:34; 12:24; Mark 3:22; Luke 11:15) and the "ruler of this world" (John 12:31; 14:30; 16:11). Paul also refers to him as the "god of this age" (2 Cor. 4:4).

The "spirit now working in the disobedient" describes how Satan works on unbelievers. They are not completely "possessed" by Satan, but they do live in the world of darkness in which Satan holds sway. He lays out the bait, and sinful people take it, disobeying God (cf. Eph. 5:6).

We followed our sinful desires. Paul calls these "fleshly desires" and "the inclinations of our flesh and thoughts" (2:3a). These passions are associated in Galatians 5:16-21 and elsewhere with sins like anger, sexual immorality, idolatry, sorcery, jealousy, strife, dissension, and drunkenness.

We may ask, did Paul get carried away here? Is our condition this bad? Yes, it is. While humans bear the image of God, and sin has not destroyed the image of God completely, we are radically depraved and unable to come to God apart from new birth (cf. John 3:3). Our behavior is explained by all three of these influences—the world, Satan, and the flesh. They all play a part in the sinful condition of humanity.

We Were Doomed (2:3b)

Paul adds to our pre-Christian condition with this dreadful statement: "We were by nature children under wrath as the others were also" (Eph. 2:3b). "The disobedient" in verse 2 are now children destined for wrath in verse 3, which is what we rightly deserved. Our spiritual status could not be more tragic or hopeless. We were justly under the judgment of God. He is right to condemn us in our sins (cf. 5:6).

God is holy, and He will not sweep sin under the rug. Many think that God in the Old Testament was a God of wrath, but God in the New Testament is soft and cuddly. Wrong. What we have now is a period of patience. The door of mercy is open wide now, and we can come into this grace and be saved. But the coming wrath of God is worse than anything in the Old Testament. The words of Hebrews should humble us: "It is a terrifying thing to fall into the hands of the living God" (Heb. 10:31).

God will act in a righteous manner, not in unrighteous revenge or in an outburst of anger. He will punish sin and sinners justly.

The good news for the Christian is that God's wrath has been poured out not on us, but on the Savior (cf. Rom. 3:21-26; 1 John 2:2). Jesus drank the cup, a metaphor that describes the wrath of God (cf. Mark 14:36). He drank the cup, and we drink grace. Bless His holy name.

Paul draws our attention to the depth of our depravity in order to magnify the mercy and grace of God in saving us, like a black cloth on which a beautiful diamond sits. And Paul gives us the diamond of the gospel with two of the sweetest words in the Bible: "**But God.**" Christian, behold your biography.

With Christ, We Are Spiritually Alive
EPHESIANS 2:4-7

God's gracious initiative and sovereign action stands in wonderful contrast to verses 1-3. We were lifeless, hopeless, and under condemnation . . . "**But God**" came to our rescue. Notice how Paul describes the character of God and the work of God in these amazing verses.

God's Character (2:4-7)

God's salvation was prompted by His **mercy, love, grace, and kindness**. Paul can in the same sentence affirm the wrath of God and the love of God. In fact, you cannot understand one without the other.

God is "rich in mercy" (Eph. 2:4). The Old Testament describes God as "abounding in faithful love" (Ps. 103:8), who "delights in faithful love" (Mic. 7:18). The word in Hebrew, *chesed*, refers to God's loyal, merciful love. God's mercy is also sovereignly distributed (cf. Rom. 9:15).

Next, God's work of salvation displays His "great love" (Eph. 2:4). To the Romans, Paul writes, "But God proves his own love for us in that while we were still sinners, Christ died for us" (Rom. 5:8).

Paul also highlights God's "grace" (2:5,8). Being made alive when we were dead is the result of the undeserved favor of God. Twelve times "grace" is mentioned in Ephesians. Paul reaches for words as he also mentions "that in the coming ages he might display the immeasurable riches of his grace through his kindness to us in Christ Jesus" (2:7). For all eternity, we will be recipients of His grace, trophies of His grace. He has displayed infinite riches of grace in kindness to us.

📖 FROM DEATH TO LIFE

The ways of the world doom us to certain spiritual death. Review the list below and circle any words that once condemned you but since have found freedom in a new life in Christ.

Fleshly desires:

lust | cursing | pornography | drug/alcohol addiction
gluttony | self-mutilation

Mental and emotional traps:

envy | pride | hate | greed | dishonesty
doubt | depression | rage | bitterness fear unforgiveness
blind ambition | laziness

Spiritual transgressions:

denying truth | teaching heresy | blasphemy

God's Work (2:5-7)

Now notice what God did in His mercy, love, and grace.

God made us alive with Christ (Eph. 2:5). The main verb that governs the paragraph, "made us alive," is introduced. Just as Jesus raised Lazarus from the dead, He also said to us, "_____ come forth!" (Insert your name, Christian!). And like Lazarus, we rise and rejoice in His grace.

I love a particular story regarding the ministry of the eighteenth-century evangelist George Whitefield, who reportedly preached on John 3 thousands of times, a text about the new birth. The evangelist was pouring out his heart one day during a Great Awakening sermon. A man with pockets stuffed with rocks came to hear him, for the purpose of physically attacking the famous evangelist once the sermon ended. But after Whitefield's emotional and powerful message, the man made his way up to the preacher, emptied his pockets, and said "I came to hear you with my pocket full of stones to break your head, but your sermon got the better of me and broke my heart."[2] Praise God that He melts the hearts of the hardest men and women and gives them new life!

There is sort of a parenthesis in verse 5: "You are saved by grace!" Paul repeats this again in verse 8: "For you are saved by grace through faith." Being raised from the dead is all of grace. Both phrases are in the perfect tense emphasizing the abiding consequences of conversion. To capture what Paul is saying we could put it like this: You have been saved (past tense), you are being saved (present tense), and you will be saved (future tense).

Notice also how Paul says that we have been made alive "with Christ" (2:5). Notice our union with Christ. In fact, all three verbs have a prefix meaning "with" (alive with Christ, raised with Christ, seated with Christ).

Consider the staggering nature of God's work in uniting us with Christ.

God raised us up with Christ (2:6a). This is a clear allusion to the resurrection of Jesus. Paul uses a compound word to declare that we have been raised together, *synergeiren*, which has this Greek prefix syn ("with"). We know this word from computers. We get the word sync from it (short for "synchronize"). The believer has been synced with Christ! What God did for Christ, He did for us. In some astonishing way, when Jesus Christ got out of the tomb two thousand years ago, Tony Merida got up with Him (cf. Col. 3:1).

God seated us with Christ (2:6b, *synekathisen*). In chapter 1 Paul praised God for exalting Jesus above all powers and forces. Now he says that we are seated with Jesus. This does not mean we are divine. There is only one on the throne. But we are seated with Him and have power to overcome. We do not have to succumb to the dark world and Satan's schemes. Also note here the "already/not yet" aspect of salvation. We are now raised and seated with Him, but we are awaiting the full completion of our salvation.

God will dispense grace forever to us in Christ (2:7). The reason God has showed us such grace is so that we might be the demonstration of His grace forever. We will be His trophies of grace. God says in effect, "Look what I can do with such a mess." Ponder the idea of grace for "ages" to come. Instead of wrath, we have everlasting grace!

In Christ, We Are God's Workmanship
EPHESIANS 2:8-10

In these final verses of the passage, Paul first emphasizes how salvation is a gift, and then how true salvation results in good works.

Salvation Is a Gift (2:8-9)

Paul first highlights **God's grace**: "For you are saved by grace through faith, and this is not from yourselves; it is God's gift—not from works, so that no one can boast." (Eph. 2:8-9).

God's great rescue of us is by grace. Think of the great reversal that has taken place between verses 1-3 and 4-7.

Dead in trespasses & sins	→	Alive together with Christ
Sons of disobedience	→	Raised up with Christ
Children of wrath	→	Seated with Christ
Children of wrath	→	Recipients of mercy
Children of wrath	→	Recipients of great love
Children of wrath	→	Recipients of rich grace
Children of wrath	→	Recipients of kindness
Children of wrath	→	Trophies of God's grace

Paul says that grace comes **through faith**. This is the human response: belief (cf. 1:13). How do we appropriate what has just been said? Faith. Faith is the instrument by which we lay hold of Christ. But faith is not a work. It is a gift. Notice what Paul says: "it is God's gift" (8b); "it" includes "faith." The whole of salvation is to be viewed as a gift. We were dead and had to be awakened to believe (cf. Acts 18:27).

There is only one who should be exalted in this salvation, and that is God. We have not worked for it and we cannot, therefore, brag about ourselves (cf. Rom. 3:27; 4:2; 1 Cor. 1:31; 4:7).

Salvation Results in Good Works (2:10)

After just saying that our works cannot save us, Paul notes the importance of works. He does not want us to think that works are unimportant. He states that works simply are not the root of our salvation. They are the fruit of salvation (cf. John 15:8; Titus 2:14). We are not saved by faith plus works, but by a faith that does work. We have a living faith, a functioning faith!

Now that we belong to God, God is working on us and in us, so that He might work through us. We are God's "workmanship" (Eph. 2:10). This word for "workmanship" (*poiema*) may be where the word poem comes from. The word was used to refer to any work of art, such as a statue, a song, architecture, a painting, or a poem.[3] Because we are God's workmanship in Christ Jesus, people should see our works and say, "That's a work of God! He did that!"

Paul adds that we were "created in Christ Jesus for good works, which God prepared ahead of time for us to do" (2:10b). Like our conversion, our spiritual growth takes place "in Christ Jesus." As we are united to Him, we have life, and that life leads to good works. Chapters 4–6 spell out what these works look like.

The reformer Martin Luther succinctly and powerfully described the relationship between faith and works:

> Faith, however, is a divine work in us. It changes us and makes us to be born anew of God (John 1); it kills the old Adam and makes altogether different men, in heart and spirit and mind and powers, and it brings with it the Holy Ghost. Oh, it is a living, busy, active, mighty thing, this faith; and so it is impossible for it not to do good works incessantly. It does not ask whether there are good works to do, but before the question rises, it has already done them, and is always at the doing of them.[4]

Indeed, the instinct of one who has new life is to do good works— at home, at work, and everywhere—to the glory of God.

Notice that these works have been "prepared ahead of time." God, in His sovereignty, had good deeds in mind when He chose us for salvation. And He planned that "we should walk in them." Notice the last line and compare it with verse 2, "in which you previously walked." This forms a bookend on the passage. We once walked in darkness, But God made us alive through faith, and now we are walking in Christ, doing good works.

Do you know this grace? If so, you can identify with John Newton, the author of "Amazing Grace," who said,

> I am not what I ought to be—ah, how imperfect and deficient! I am not what I wish to be—I abhor what is evil, and I would cleave to what is good! I am not what I hope to be—soon, soon shall I put off mortality, and with mortality all sin and imperfection. Yet, though I am not what I ought to be, nor what I wish to be, nor what I hope to be, I can truly say, I am not what I once was; a slave to sin and Satan; and I can heartily join with the apostle, and acknowledge, 'By the grace of God I am what I am.'[5]

Let us never lose the wonder of God's saving grace.

CALLED TO DO GOOD WORKS

God has good works planned for you, and you don't need to think long or hard to discover some of them. See the questions below for examples of common good works. The first one has been done for you. If you are not sure of your response, try prayer and soul searching.

Are you married? God plans for you to do this good work: <u>Be a faithful, loving spouse.</u>

Are you a parent? God plans for you to do this good work:

Are you employed? God plans for you to do this good work:

Do you have neighbors? God plans for you to do this good work:

Are you a member of a church? (You should be!) God plans for you to do this good work:

Can you perform a random act of kindness? God plans for you to do this good work:

Are you able to engage in philanthropy? God plans for you to do this good work:

A CLOSER LOOK

Regeneration

How are we "made alive," or "born again," or what we call the doctrine of regeneration?

We have what theologians have termed an "outer call," which goes out to everyone through the proclamation of the gospel, and "an inner call," which the Holy Spirit does in hearts. Those who are Christians have sensed this inner calling (Gal. 1:6). Paul experienced this call to come to Christ (Gal. 1:15).

We cannot overemphasize the importance of this doctrine of regeneration. Christianity is not about becoming a nicer person, nor is it about starting a new religious routine. It is about becoming a new person (2 Cor. 5:17).

One night a religious man named Nicodemus came to ask Jesus some spiritual questions. He had a lot of religious knowledge, but he had not been made alive. Jesus told him, "Truly I tell you, unless someone is born again, he cannot see the kingdom of God" (John 3:3).

Peter tells us the means by which God brings the dead to life: "You have been born again—not of perishable seed but of imperishable—through the living and enduring word of God" (1 Pet. 1:23). When the gospel is preached, God by His Spirit awakens hearts to repent and trust in Christ.

ower (Commercial) Agora, next to the theater, at Ephesus.

PERSONAL REFLECTION

1. How does Paul describe our pre-Christian status in 2:1-3?

2. Why are the words "But God" so sweet?

3. How does this passage teach our union with Christ?

4. What is the believer's future? How should this impact our daily lives?

1. Hughes, R. K. (1990). *Ephesians: The Mystery of the Body of Christ.* Preaching the Word (Wheaton, IL: Crossway, 1990), 66.
2. John Dunn, *The Great Evangelical Awakening of the 18th Century* (Blackwood, South Austral.: New Creation Publications Inc., 1983), 17, https://www.newcreationlibrary.org.au/books/pdf/072_GreatAwakening.pdf.
3. Hughes, *Ephesians*, 82.
4. Martin Luther, *Commentary on Romans.* Translated by J. Theodore Mueller (Grand Rapids: Kregel, 1954), xvii.
5. John Newton, *The Christian Spectator.* Volume 3. (New Haven: Converse, 1821.) 186.

WE ARE MEMBERS OF GOD'S HOUSEHOLD

EPHESIANS 2:11-22

I n this important passage on the nature of the church, Paul reminds believers of their prior alienation from God and His people, and what Christ has done to reconcile them to God and to one another. New Testament scholar Kline Snodgrass says that this is "perhaps the single most significant ecclesiological text in the New Testament."[1]

We regularly need a renewed vision of the church, seeing it from the New Testament's perspective, so that we can appreciate the church's centrality, it's glory, and our responsibility in it. I appreciate the following story from Alistair Begg which magnifies the place of the church in the world:

> In the 1920's, Lord Reith helped to establish the BBC—the British Broadcasting Corporation—and then from 1927 served as its first Director-General. He was a somewhat severe man from the highlands of Scotland. As the BBC began to be carried along by the tide of secularism that swept through Britain in the sixties, a young producer stood up in a meeting and said to Lord Reith that the world was changing, and that the BBC did not need to continue with its religious programming output.
>
> People were no longer interested in it, he said, and the church was becoming increasingly obsolete.
>
> Lord Reith, who was 6'6 tall, stood up, told this young man to take a seat, and said: "The church will stand at the grave of the BBC."[2]

Indeed, it will. It will stand when all news outlets die. It will stand when every organization and institution and empire come to an end! It is Jesus's church. He declared "I will build my church, and the gates of Hades will not overpower it." (Matt. 16:18). What a privilege to belong to the church!

This passage shows us that Christians—by grace—have a people to whom we belong. This communal identity is given beautifully in Ephesians 2:19-22. But before we get there, Paul reminds the believers of their prior **alienation**, and what Christ has done to **reconcile** them to God and one another. We should "remember" (2:11) what God has done for us in Christ, so that we may live with an appropriate sense of grace and gratitude before God and within our local church fellowship.

Alienation: Who We Once Were
EPHESIANS 2:11-12

Verses 11-12 follow the pattern of verses 1-3. They tell us the dark picture of what life apart from Christ involves.

Paul addresses the readers by saying, "you were Gentiles in the flesh" (Eph. 2:11). He is highlighting a real physical difference between Gentile and Jew. But he goes on to note that this physical difference is of no ultimate significance in terms of creating unity, for our unity is found in Christ.

The Jews looked on the Gentiles as "uncircumcised," lacking the physical sign of their covenant with the Lord. They viewed the uncircumcised as being separated from the Lord. But Paul says that this practice is something simply "done in the flesh by human hands" (2:11) in order to drive home the point that it belonged to the old order of Judaism with its external features; but now "what matters instead is a new creation" (Gal. 6:15).

Paul goes on to elaborate on the pre-Christian past of the Gentiles.

Christ-less (2:12a)

They were "without Christ" (Eph. 2:12a); that is, the Gentiles were separated from the Messianic hope of Israel (cf. Rom. 9:4-5). True, some Jews were and still are separated from Christ, but they have been told in their Scriptures of Messiah (cf. Rom. 3:2). The Gentiles were foreigners to these things.

There is nothing worse than being separated from Christ. And there is nothing greater than being united to Christ! Never forget what God has done for you through the Messiah.

Foreigners (2:12b)

Prior to their conversion, Paul says the Gentile unbelievers in Ephesus were "excluded from the citizenship of Israel, and foreigners to the covenants of promise" (Eph. 2:12b). They were alienated from God's people.

Prior to conversion, Gentile unbelievers were foreigners to the covenant people (2:19). The term "covenants" implies a series of covenants: Abraham (Gen. 15:7-21; 17:1-21), Isaac (Gen. 26:2-5), Jacob (Gen. 28:13-15), Israel (Ex. 24:1-8), and David (2 Sam. 7). The phrase "promise" probably has to do with God's promise to Abraham. To be separated from the covenants of promise meant they were missing the covenants that promised the Messiah (cf. Rom. 9:4).

Hopeless and Godless (2:12c)

Further, Paul states that they were "without hope and without God in the world" (Eph. 2:12c). While God did plan on blessing all nations through Israel, the Gentile unbelievers did not know this. Because they did not know the promises, they did not have the hope of the promises, nor did they know the God of the promises. They had opted for idols instead of God, suppressing the truth revealed to them (Rom. 1:18-23). Because they did not know God, they did not know hope.

Let us remember, before we trusted in Christ for salvation we were in the same tragic position. We were separated from God and His people. You at one time were separated from Christ and gospel community. If we continue to remember where we came from, we will live with constant gratitude toward God and love toward His people.

Reconciliation: What Christ Has Done
EPHESIANS 2:13-18

As in Ephesians 2:4, there is another great "but" statement. A dramatic change has occurred. "But now in Christ Jesus, you who were far away have been brought near by the blood of the Christ" (Eph. 2: 13). It is by the blood of Christ that we can be brought near to God. Only by His blood can we be reconciled to God.

So the cross is central. Apart from the work of Christ, there is no salvation and there is no church. And the church must always keep the message of the crucified (and risen) Christ central in its proclamation, otherwise we are more like a social club than a church.

After saying Christ's death has brought us near, Paul goes on to add more results of Christ's sacrifice. The verbs in this section emphasize what Christ has done in order to reverse our condition: "made one," "tore down," "made of no effect," "create," "reconcile," and "proclaimed." What a Savior!

Paul also shifts from "you" to "we" and "our" in this section. Both Jew and Gentile have the same hope: Christ's atoning death. Consider three things the Savior has done for "us" through His reconciling work on the cross.

Christ Has Brought Us Peace (2:14a)

Jesus has brought us peace with God and others. Jesus is the ultimate peacemaker. "For He is our peace," Paul says. Peace is found in a person, Jesus. This peace was promised in the Old Testament (e.g., Isa. 9:6; Mic. 5:5), affirmed in the Gospels (e.g., Luke 1:79; 2:14; 19:42; John 14:27), and explained in the Epistles (Rom. 5:1; Col. 1:20; 3:15).

Christ Has Made Us One (2:14b-16)

Paul says that Jesus "tore down the dividing wall" (Eph. 14b). Christ's blood has obliterated this old, long-standing division between Jew and Gentile. "In His flesh" Jesus tore down the wall that separated these groups, that is, through His atoning work on the cross.

While Paul could be referring to a literal wall in the temple, it seems more likely that he is referring to the barrier of "the law consisting of commands and expressed in regulations," that is, the ceremonial law (2:15a). The parallel passage in Colossians 2:11 and 16-21 alludes to circumcision, questions about food and drink, and regulations about festivals, new moons, and the Sabbath. These commandments as regulations put up a huge wall between Jew and Gentile. Jesus set all of this aside by dying on the cross. At the cross, Jesus fulfilled all the shadows and types of the ceremonial system.

As a result, Christ created "in Himself one new man from the two, resulting in peace" (2:15b). Jesus's abolishing of something old has led to something new: one new humanity. Christ has created one new man. It is not as though Gentiles have been transformed into Jews or vice versa, but rather God has created one new man.

People still like to make walls today, but the gospel brings unity like nothing else (cf. Gal. 3:28; Col. 3:11). The Jew/Gentile rivalry was intense. It was religious. The Gentiles did not know the God of Israel. It was cultural. Jews had rituals, feasts, and ceremonies that distinguished them from the

📖 BRINGING US TOGETHER

The Bible is filled with examples of how Christianity brings people who seemed natural enemies into fellowship. See the passages below to identify the unlikely pairs.

Joshua 2: The spies and _____.

1 Kings 17:7-16: Elijah and _____.

1 Samuel 18: David and _____.

Luke 19:1-10 Jesus and _____.

Acts 15: Paul and _____

nations. It was racial. The Jews could boast of having the blood of Abraham flowing through their veins. Yet, through Christ, these two enemies have become friends.

Paul elaborates on this idea, speaking of the double reconciliation that has taken place through the work of Christ: "He did this so that he might reconcile both to God in one body through the cross by which he put the hostility to death" (Eph. 2:16). Notice, the hostility has been put to death. As Stott says, "God turned away his own wrath, and we, seeing his great love, turned away ours also."[3] The hostility has come to an end through the death of Jesus. The best antidote to disunity and hostility between believers is a fresh comprehension of the cross of Christ.

Christ Preached Peace (2:17)

The cross of Christ is how our peace was achieved, but now it is to be announced (Eph. 2:17). Commentators debate if this refers to Jesus's earthly ministry of preaching, the crucifixion itself (as a symbol of proclaiming peace), His postresurrection proclamation of peace (John 20:19-21), or the ongoing proclamation through the apostles and now through the church. I am not sure it has to be limited to any of these. Jesus certainly proclaimed the gospel of peace before the cross, on the cross, and after the resurrection.

And now the followers of Jesus must be ready to preach the gospel of peace (Eph. 6:15). We are to tell the world how people can have peace with God.

Paul adds that this good news was preached to those "far away" and those "who were near"—that is, to Gentile and Jew (cf. Isa. 57:19). The whole world needs this gospel. Let us be faithful to share it.

Christ Has Given Us Access to God (2:18)

Those who respond to Jesus's work and message now have access to God. Notice the Trinitarian language: Paul says it is "through Him [Christ] we both have access in one spirit to the Father" (Eph. 2:18).

This is what prayer is about. The ongoing benefit of Christ's reconciliation is that we today have access to God. We can now come to God with boldness (3:12) because of what Christ has done. Tim Keller writes, "The only person who dares wake up a king at 3:00am for a glass of water is a child of the King. We have that kind of access."[4] But this is not just a personal privilege, it's also a corporate privilege. We "both" have access to God. When the community of faith is joined together in prayer, saying, "Our Father in heaven" (Matt. 6:9), it is the result of the work of Jesus on our behalf.

Identification: Who We Have Now Become
EPHESIANS 2:19-22

Paul summarizes Christ's reconciling work by reminding the Gentiles of who they now are. In Ephesians 2:5-6 I noted the three "with" (syn) words that show how we have been synced with Christ. In 2:19-22 there are three more "with" or "together" words: *sympolitai* ("fellow citizens"); *synarmologeo* ("put together"); and *synoikodomeo* ("built together").[5] These words emphasize that we have been synced not only to Christ, but to other Christians. To press home his point, Paul uses three word pictures: citizens, family, and stones in a temple.

📖 BELONGING

If you are tempted to take for granted what it means to be a member of God's household, let these verses be striking reminders that Christ reserved special places for and took special care of His people.

Read the passages below to identify the focus of each. Circle the verses that hold special promise for you.

Deuteronomy 7:6

Psalm 68:6

Psalm 147:3

Jeremiah 1:5

Matthew 19:14

Citizens of God's Kingdom (2:19a)

First, Paul says that the Gentiles are no longer refugees; now they have a citizenship. The Gentile believers are not second-class citizens in someone else's territory. They are full members of the kingdom.

Paul is writing during a time in which Roman citizenship was prized. Roman citizens had wonderful privileges. Citizenship in a great country is a blessing, but there is nothing like being a citizen of the kingdom of God (cf. Phil. 3:20).

Foreigners in another city or country feel vulnerable. But Paul says we do not have to feel this way. We belong. We are part of a kingdom that has no end, the only kingdom that has no end.

I have always appreciated in presidential addresses, when the president begins by saying, "My fellow Americans." I may or may not like his following speech, nor his policies, but I have always loved that moment. "He's talking to me. I'm an American." There is a sense of gratitude that I feel. But imagine Jesus Christ saying to us all, "My fellow citizens of the kingdom of God." And yet, He does. If you are in Christ, you really are a full citizen, with all the privileges that come with that. Praise God for His grace!

Members of God's Family (2:19b)

Paul's metaphor of God's new community changes to something more personal: a family. One might imagine Jew and Gentile together in one kingdom, but to be one family is stunning (cf. 1 Tim. 3:15).

How are we one family? We have the same Father. Paul just made that point in 2:18. We are adopted children, as Paul asserted in 1:5. The church is made up of adopted brothers and sisters. We have responsibilities in the family. We are one family, each fulfilling his or her role, bringing glory to our Father (Eph. 5:1). In 1 Timothy 5:1-2 Paul says that we should treat one another like family.

My adopted son Joshua, born in Ethiopia, had been home with us for about four months when he experienced his first Christmas. After being amazed by the snow in Northern Virginia, we entered Joshua's new grandparents' home. The house was filled with family members. Joshua, who was five years old at the time, was holding my hand as he carefully observed all of these cousins, aunts, uncles, and grandparents. With the Christmas music playing, lights shining, and presents under the tree (for him too!), he looked up and asked, "Papa, are all of these people our family?" "Yes son," I said, "all of these people are our family." Likewise, every time we walk into our church's large or small gatherings we can say of fellow believers, "All of these people are our family." Some of you may be tempted to say in your family gatherings, "Unfortunately, all of these people are our family!" But this too illustrates the church! Every church has people who are difficult to love. You may be one of them from time to time. But that's the church. What Joshua was learning during his first Christmas was this lesson: when you get adopted, you get a new family.[6]

The church is not a building we go to or an event we attend (as important as these are). The church is family to whom you belong. Be careful not to treat the church as a hotel—visiting a place occasionally, giving a tip if you are served well. Rather, see the church as part of your Christian identity, and understand that we all have a role in God's household.

Stones in God's Temple (2:20-22)

Paul's third metaphor would have been very vivid for his audience. For nearly one thousand years, the temple had been a focal point of Israel—from Solomon to Zerubbabel to Herod. Now there was a new temple, made up of people.

In verse 20, Paul says that the foundation of the temple is God's Word. The apostles and prophets were teachers, and what Paul is emphasizing here is their teaching. This emphasis should not surprise us. The church stands or falls based on its faithfulness to God's Word (cf. Acts 2:42).

Next, we see the cornerstone mentioned. There is only one cornerstone: Jesus. He makes the whole building possible. He is what the whole community is built on. He gives security to the building, and He gives it alignment. While the apostles' teaching is being emphasized, Jesus's person and work is also being emphasized. Jesus is also how the church grows and is held together. There is no unity or growth if Christ is not the cornerstone.

Paul likens the people to stones. He says that in the Lord, "You also are being built together for God's dwelling." Peter says something like this as well, calling us "living stones" (1 Pet. 2:5). We are carefully shaped building blocks, fitted to build this temple. Each new member is added to it.

By saying, "you also," Paul is referring to the Gentiles being added to this building. Previously the Gentiles were not allowed to enter the temple, but now they are a part of it!

Notice it is "in the Lord" (2:21) that we are a dwelling place for God by the Spirit. Through Christ, by the Spirit of God, God dwells in us personally and as a community. Ultimately, this reality will be fully realized and enjoyed in the New Heavens and New Earth, when God makes His dwelling place with man.

A great temple stood in Ephesus (the temple of Artemis). In Jerusalem they had a great temple. But Paul says, through Christ, by the Spirit, there is a better temple; it is made up of people from every tribe and tongue. We are joined together and built together. Each one is related to the other in a special way, and we are all growing together in Christ.

aining Ruins of the Temple of Artemis

A CLOSER LOOK

Loving Our Church Family

An obvious implication from these three pictures is that Christ wants to create a people, not merely isolated individuals who believe in Him. This passage confronts Western individualism. To be separate from the church is to say, "I want to be a stone apart from a building" or "a son or daughter separated from my family" or "a refugee away from my country." This is how God intends for us to live out our faith and love one another: in community. It is an incredible gift of God's grace to have a family of faith. All these privileges have come to us via the cross-work of Jesus Christ.

There are several reasons people aren't deeply invested in a church family.[7] Regardless of the reasons, we all benefit from recapturing the New Testament's vision of Christ's church, and Ephesians 2:11-22 is a wonderful text to help do just that. (And Paul has more important things to say about the church in the following chapters of Ephesians). Hopefully, a fresh, prayerful look at Ephesians 2:11-22 will inspire us to love our churches more faithfully.

Architectural fragments, statues, and reliefs gathered from the ruins of Ephesus. Most prominent is the statue of Artemis, the primary goddess of the city. The Temple of Artemis at Ephesus was one of the seven wonders of the ancient world.

ILLUSTRATOR PHOTO/MURRAY SEVE

PERSONAL REFLECTION

1. From this passage explain what Christ has done for us.

2. How does verse 18 relate to prayer? How should it affect our view of prayer?

3. Which of the three illustrations of the church in 2:19-22—citizens, family, or stones—made the biggest impact on you? Why?

4. How should this passage change the way we think about the church?

1. Klyne Snodgrass, *Ephesians.* The NIV Application Commentary (Grand Rapids: Zondervan, 1996), 123.
2. Alistair Begg, *Brave by Faith* (The Good Book Company, 2021), 43.
3. John R. W. Stott, *God's New Society: The Message of Ephesians,* The Bible Speaks Today. (Downers Grove, IL: InterVarsity Press, 1979), 102.
4. Tim Keller, Quote on Twitter (@timkellernyc) Feb 23, 2015. https://twitter.com/timkellernyc/status/569890726349307904?lang=en.
5. Snodgrass, *Ephesians*, 136.
6. Tony Merida, *Love Your Church* (The Good Book Company, 2021), 16–17.
7. Some reasons are stated in Tony Merida, *Love Your Church*, 20–21.

WE ARE RECONCILED TO OTHERS

EPHESIANS 3:1-21

Have you ever been interrupted in prayer? Many things can cause this—babies crying, microwaves dinging, phones buzzing, doorbells ringing, or sirens sounding. Sometimes our wandering mind just goes elsewhere.

Paul appears to begin an intercessory prayer for the church in Ephesians 3:1, but then he goes on a holy rabbit trail and does not pick up the actual prayer until 3:14. This digression occurs as he gets overwhelmed by the grace of Jesus, and His ministry to the Gentiles. But I'm glad he includes this parenthetical material because it is important and edifying! Paul speaks of his sufferings, the incorporation of the Gentiles into the people of God, the cosmic nature of the church, the proclamation of the riches of Christ, and the believers' access to God.

Proclaiming Christ
EPHESIANS 3:1-13

The Prisoner of Christ (3:1,13)

Paul opens and closes this passage by speaking of his present condition and the associated sufferings (Eph. 3:1,13). His imprisonment shows the nature of a Christian missionary. Jesus called Paul to a special ministry; that ministry involved suffering (Acts 9:15-16). Paul was willing to suffer on behalf of Christ, for the sake of the mission (Col. 1:24).

Strikingly, in verse 1 Paul does not refer to himself as a prisoner of Caesar, but "of Christ Jesus." The will of Christ took Paul to prison. He knew that he was not imprisoned because of some moral lapse or because he had displeased God in some way; it was because of his sacrificial commitment to the will of Jesus that he was chained to a Roman soldier, writing this letter from prison.

Verse 13 speaks of the loving, pastoral heart of Paul. He is the one in prison, yet he appears to want to set the people's mind at ease. He tells his readers/hearers that they should not be overly discouraged by his situation, but to realize God's purposes are being fulfilled and those purposes are for their good.

The Message of Christ (3:2-6)

Paul speaks now of the responsibility that he has to communicate the message of Christ, and he expresses his desire for the church to understand this message (Eph. 3:2-3).

It should go without saying that missionaries are called not only to go, but they are to go with the right message. Lots of false religions have missionaries. What makes Christian missions distinct is the message about the crucified, risen, reigning, and returning King. We must make sure, as missionaries, that we are not exporting a deficient gospel.

Paul had a unique role in redemptive history. He was given "insight about the mystery of Christ" (3:4). As God's steward, Paul's responsibility involved explaining God's intent to create a special people, made up of both Jew and Gentile through Christ (3:5-6). Paul's role was to explain this "mystery," and the church's role is to "understand" it (3:4) and then communicate it also.

This "mystery" was not like Ephesian mystery cults. It was not a mystery of esoteric knowledge, reserved for a secret few. This mystery, this message about Christ, is for all nations. This mystery can be understood. While the plan of God was present in the Old Testament, parts were unclear or "hidden" in a sense (3:9). But when Christ appeared, the lights came on, clarifying the nature of the gospel and its benefits.

The Grace to Proclaim Christ (3:7-8a)

God's grace in Christ had a humbling effect on Paul, and it also had an empowering effect.

Because Paul understood grace, he lived with a profound sense of humble gratitude to God. He knew that apart from grace, he would not be doing what he was. So he says, "grace was given to me" twice (Eph. 3:7,8). He deflects attention away from himself, toward the proper place of praise: the God of all grace.

Notice how Paul refers to himself as "the least of all the saints" (3:8). He feels privileged to serve the King. Do you? We do not have to serve Jesus; we get to serve Jesus. Notice how Paul refers to himself as a humble "servant of this gospel" (3:7). Even though he is an inspired apostle, Paul knows he is a servant of Jesus.

We should realize that we need God's grace to empower us, as well. Paul ties "grace" and "power" together in verse 7. Paul shows us that the mighty power of God (1:19-20) provides sufficient strength for weak, fragile, ordinary people as they make the glories of Christ known.

The Incalculable Riches of Christ (3:8b-9)

Paul now provides the purposes of God's enabling grace.

First, God empowered Paul to proclaim the incalculable riches of Christ. This particular word (incalculable) appears nowhere outside of biblical Greek. When Paul thought about the glory of Christ, he made up a

📖 A PRISONER OF JESUS CHRIST

In the space below, list the five most pressing circumstances of your life that seem to contain or confine you—for example, caring for an aging parent. Put a N beside those you believe are outside of His will for your life. Put a Y beside each of those that you understand to be under God's control. Circle the circumstance you find the most challenging and write this directive below: this could be your finest hour.

Circumstance	God's Will	God's Control
1)		
2)		
3)		
4)		
5)		

word! One scholar notes that this word is built on the word for "footprint." That word was used literally in Greek literature for a tracker, someone who pursues another by following footprints. It has the sense then of "tracing out" or "searching." We will always be exploring the depth and wonder of our Lord Jesus.

Don't miss the fact that Paul's all-consuming subject of proclamation is a person: Christ. Is Christ the all-consuming subject of your teaching and preaching?

Second, Paul also received grace in order to explain the global nature of God's plan of salvation. He was sent to "shed light for all about the administration of the mystery hidden for ages in God who created all things" (Eph. 3:9). He had the great task of illuminating God's plan to believers; specifically, how the Jew and Gentile are one in Christ. This plan was not an afterthought, but part of the God's divine plan.

Finally, God empowered Paul to make known God's manifold wisdom through the church (3:10-12). He says that the church—made up of Jew and Gentile—is making known the manifold wisdom of God to "the rulers and authorities in the heavens" (3:10). It seems to me that the angels look on at grace and marvel while demonic forces look on in fear and tremble. The existence of the church is announcing to these dark forces that their influence is coming to an end once and for all.

Notice that God intends to make His plan known to them through the church. There is more going on with the church than meets the eye. If you are part of the church, then you are part of a cosmic sermon that is being preached to spiritual rulers and authorities. Christ is the central character in this plan (3:11).

One of the gifts of living in this present age is that believers in Christ's church can experience a nearness to God that far exceeds that of the old covenant. Christians can boldly approach God because of Christ: "In him we have boldness and confident access through faith in him" (3:12). We can come freely and openly to God because of what Christ has done for us. This is just one of the many "riches" that we have received from our Savior.

Praying for Power
EPHESIANS 3:14-21

Having given us a compelling vision of a Christ-centered missionary, Paul now prays for God to empower the Ephesian believers and for God to grant them a greater knowledge of His extraordinary love for them. Let me make three applications from this marvelous prayer.

1. Pray with Humility (3:14-16)

Consider Paul's posture: kneeling. Whenever someone is kneeling in prayer in the Bible, they are indicating deep humility and deep emotion before God. I do not want to suggest that this is the only correct posture for prayer, for we have people praying in all kinds of postures in the Bible, but I do want to emphasize the heart of the idea of kneeling.

Humble Gratitude (3:14) Paul begins by saying "For this reason" (Eph. 3:14). What prompted this prayer? What was the "reason"? Paul began this prayer in verse 1 but never got to his prayer. So, what preceded 3:1? Two chapters of God's amazing grace! Gratitude for the grace of God in chapters 1–2 prompted this prayer in chapter 3.

When we reflect on God's amazing grace, it should lead us to get on our face before God, who called us, adopted us, redeemed us, and forgave us. Christ died on our behalf. The Spirit has sealed us. God has brought us from death to life, has raised us with Christ, and has seated us with Christ. God has made us part of His church. In light of these realities, we bow in gratitude.

Humble Desperation (3:14-16) Kneeling is also a sign of desperation. When we realize that we are approaching the only One who can act on our behalf, it gives us a proper sense of helplessness.

Why is Paul so passionate and desperate in Ephesians 3:14? I think because he knows the Ephesians need something that can only come from God: power. Notice how Paul prays that God would "grant" them to be strengthened (3:16). He knew God's power was a gift. So he was desperate for God to answer, and so should we be.

Humble Confidence (3:14-16) Paul's introduction here shows us that we should also come before God with confidence. We can pray with confidence because of our position in Christ (cf. 2:18; 3:12), knowing that we are bowing before the "Father" who loves us (3:14).

Our Father is the sovereign Father. Here Paul says that "every family in heaven and on earth is named" from Him. This is an expression of the Father's authority and rule over all.

Our Father is rich and powerful. Paul prays for God to answer "according to the riches of His glory." God's resources never run out. Therefore, bring your petitions to Him confidently.

Our Father is gracious. Paul asks for God to "grant" the church strength. God loves to give good gifts to His children, particularly those things pertaining to the Spirit—not just material blessings but the Spirit's guidance and work (cf. Luke 11:11-13).

2. Pray for the Fullness of God's Power and Love (3:16-19)

As we move to Paul's petitions, notice the two main requests: power and love. Verse 19b summarizes these requests climactically, as Paul asks for God to fill the believers "with all the fullness of God." We begin with the lead request "to be strengthened with power" (Eph. 3:16); then we move through the next requests (notice the use of "that") until we reach the apex in verse 19.

Notice all the phrases about power and love:
- "strengthened with power" (3:16)
- "rooted and firmly established in love" (3:17b)
- "able to comprehend [God's love]" (3:18)
- "to know the Christ's love" (3:19)
- "filled with all the fullness of God" (3:19)

Paul is essentially praying for the readers to experience what he has just talked about in the previous chapters: Christ's supreme power and God's great love toward sinners.

We Need to Be Strengthened by the Spirit's Power (3:16-17a). Paul asks God to strengthen the believers with power in their "inner being" (3:16; 2 Cor. 4:16). We need strength and power on the inside. This is how we fight sin, proclaim the gospel with courage, and love people the way Christ has loved us.

Why do we need to be strengthened by the Spirit in the inner man? Paul says, "that Christ may dwell in your hearts through faith" (3:17a). It is indeed part of God's redemptive plan that Christ dwells in believers, not in a tabernacle or temple.

But Paul is speaking about something more than just Christ dwelling in our hearts. Paul is talking about Christ ruling in the heart. Paul's choice of words for "dwell" is important. He uses a strong word. He could use the word that means to "inhabit" but instead he uses the word that means to "settle down." It carries the idea of a permanent resident, not a short-lived resident.

We Need Power to Grasp Christ's Love (3:17b-19a). Paul moves on to express his desire for the Ephesians to know more of Christ's love for them. Paul apparently thinks that they do not appreciate Christ's love as they should. It is not a mere intellectual appreciation of the love of Christ that Paul is after. He wants them to experience this love more fully.

God's love is rooted in history, most magnificently at the cross, but that love is to be tasted. It is to be experienced (cf. 1 Pet. 1:8). Paul says that this love "surpasses knowledge" (Eph. 3:19). It is a love that is knowable and explainable to a degree, yet it must be experienced.

Paul points out four aspects of love that we need to know more.

First, know that you are secured in God's love (3:17b). Paul describes Christians as "being rooted and firmly established in love." Our lives are to be built on the foundation of Christ's love, and all spiritual fruit grows from the soil of His love.

Dear saint, let your roots go down into the love of Christ and draw strength from there, living moment by moment knowing you are loved by God. This love has come to us before the foundation of the world (1:3-6). In love, God has called us and brought us to life (2:4-5).

Second, know more about the limitless dimensions of God's love (3:18). Paul uses the expressions: "length and width, height and depth" to describe God's love (3:17; cf. Rom. 8:31-39). It is difficult to understand precisely what Paul is getting at, but God's love is certainly all these descriptions! Scripture speaks of the breadth of God's love in that He has included all races as part of His family; Jew and Gentile are one. Scripture speaks of His love being as long as eternity (Jer. 31:3). Scripture speaks of God's love being higher than the heavens (Ps. 103:11-12). Scripture speaks of His love in terms of depth in that God casts our sins into the bottom of the sea (Mic. 7:19).

Notice that we should try to "comprehend" it (Eph. 3:18). But it takes God's power to do so! Notice also that we should try to grasp it "with all the saints" (3:18). All the saints should think on the love of Christ together. Discuss His love; share stories of His love; study the Bible together. This is another reference to the importance of the church. God intends to shape us through community as we reflect on His gospel. We are not intended to live the Christian life in isolation.

Third, know more about this love that surpasses knowledge (3:19a). Paul urges us to grasp and experience God's love as much as possible. We cannot get to the bottom of God's love since it "surpasses knowledge" (3:19). But let us press on to know as much as we can so that we may appreciate it more deeply and live in light of it more faithfully. Knowing more about God's love will make us more passionate worshipers and more loving and forgiving individuals. Further, as we grow in our knowledge of His love together, the more unified and hospitable our churches will be.

Finally, know more of God's love that you may grow more mature (3:19b). Paul concludes his prayer with this great phrase: "Filled with all the fullness of God" (3:19b). Paul wants them to know the love of God in Christ to the end that they might "be all that God wants them to be" or "be spiritually mature."[1] Paul uses a similar expression in 4:13 to talk about spiritual maturity.

3. Pray with Great Expectations (3:20-21)

Paul concludes his prayer with praise. He shows us the greatness of God. Consider the "what," "how," and "why" of this doxology.

What? Paul says God is "able" (Eph. 3:20a)! Able to do what? He is able "to do above and beyond all that we ask or think" (3:20a).

God can do more in response to one prayer than we can do in one hundred years of planning and plodding. Do we believe God alone is the only Sovereign? He is the one who raised Jesus from the dead and placed Him as head over the church, and he has put all things under his feet! If so, then pour out your heart to Him, believing that He is able.

We need a vision of God that increases our faith in God's greatness. The best way to do this is to fill our minds with the Word of God.

How? How does God work beyond our imagination? Paul says it is "according to the power that works *in us*" (3:20b; emphasis added). Think about the examples of this in the Bible. Think of His work in the life of Abraham, Moses, Gideon, David, Elijah, Isaiah, Nehemiah, the disciples, and the church. God can do extraordinary things through ordinary people by His power at work within them.

Why? Why does God do these things? Paul says it in verse 21. This should be the ultimate goal for our prayers for power and love: "To Him be glory in the church and in Christ Jesus to all generations, forever and ever. Amen." God blesses His people for His own glory.

But notice Paul says that God desires His glory in the church and in Christ Jesus. John Stott says, "God desires glory in the bride and in the bridegroom; in the community of peace, and in the Peacemaker."[2]

For how long? Forever. God is worthy of all glory in "all generations" to come and throughout all eternity. Forever, God will be glorified for His power and love. Forever, God will be glorified by His people. Forever, God will be glorified in Christ Jesus. Amen.

PERSONAL REFLECTION

1. Why is it right to say that the riches of Christ are "incalculable"? (3:8)

2. What prompts Paul to pray with such humility and gratitude? (3:14)

3. For what does Paul pray? Pause and pray through these petitions. (3:16-19)

1. D. A. Carson, *Praying with Paul*. Second Edition (Grand Rapids: Baker, 2014). 172.
2. John R. W. Stott, *God's New Society: The Message of Ephesians,* The Bible Speaks Today. (Downers Grove, IL: InterVarsity Press, 1979), 141.

┌─ **A CLOSER LOOK** ─────────────────────────────────

World Missions (3:1-13)

Paul's holy digression serves as a "missions text." Like the parallel text in Colossians 1:24-29, it contains missional language. We read of the Gentiles or "nations" (Eph. 3:1,6,8; see Col. 1:27-28), suffering for the sake of the mission (Eph. 3:1; see Col 1:24), the administration of grace given (Eph. 3:2; see Col. 1:25), the revelation of the mystery or the plan of God (Eph. 3:4-6; see Col. 1:26-27), and the proclamation of Christ who is at the center of the plan (Eph. 3:8; Col. 1:28). This passage is saturated with Paul's passion for the nations to worship the reigning Christ.

If someone asks you, "Where did you get your passion for missions?" a proper response is "from the Bible." From cover to cover, there is a missions thrust in the Bible because there is a Messianic thrust in the Bible.

THE SPIRIT OF PRAYER

Train yourself to focus your prayers for others on the spiritual as well as physical, financial, emotional, etc. First, make a mental list of people on your heart today for whatever reason. Then insert their names in the spaces below. Pray this prayer, perhaps kneeling at your seat, for your loved ones and consider whether you have served them well.

I pray that he may grant _____, according to the riches of his glory, to be strengthened with power in _____'s inner being through his Spirit.

I pray that Christ may dwell in _____'s heart through faith.

I pray that _____, being rooted and firmly established in love, may be able to comprehend with all the saints what is the length and width, height and depth of God's love.

I pray that _____ will know Christ's love that surpasses knowledge.

I pray that _____ may be filled with all the fullness of God.

WE ARE UNIFIED IN THE CHURCH

EPHESIANS 4:1-16

If your church is anything like ours, you have a lot of health-conscious individuals in the fellowship. We have nurses, doctors, pharmacists, fitness center coaches, coaches of various sports, athletes, and generally speaking, a lot of people interested in fitness, recreation, and healthy living.

In Ephesians 4, Paul describes another body, the body of Christ. We should be even more interested in the health of this body.

We should think carefully about Paul's teaching here, for we, as Christians, are part of this body. And we should pay attention because, unlike a lot of changing health opinions, this is eternal truth. I am not certain about the benefit of parsley water, kale smoothies, quinoa salads, or creatine, but I am sure about the apostle's instruction. This plan will do a body good.

So what is the nature of a healthy body of Christ, and how should it function? Having already laid out some important theological truths about the church (Eph. 1:22-23; 2:11-22; 3:10), Paul shows us what the church looks like in practice. We can trace Paul's teaching by noting **three marks of a healthy church**: (1) spiritual unity, (2) spiritual diversity, and (3) spiritual maturity.

A Healthy Church Is Marked by Spiritual Unity
EPHESIANS 4:1-6

United by Divine Calling (4:1)

Paul says, "Therefore I, the prisoner for the Lord, urge you to walk worthy of the calling you have received" (Eph. 4:1). The word "therefore" introduces us to the second half of the letter (chapters 4–6), one that will be filled with practical exhortations, based on the theology of the previous three chapters.

The word walk is important. It essentially means, "to conduct one's life." After Paul has expounded the gospel in the first three chapters, he now wants his readers to know how they are to conduct their lives in a way that is in keeping with the gospel.

This idea of "calling" goes back to the beginning of the book. God has called us to Himself by His grace. Now we are to live worthy of that privileged calling, by reflecting the character of Christ. Paul says this calling is for every Christian, not just professional clergy or the "elite forces Christians."

Paul illustrates what a worthy walk looks like in his own situation. He is a "prisoner for the Lord" (4:1; cf. 3:1). He has surrendered his life to the lordship of Christ, and it has taken him to prison. While you may not be sent to prison for obeying Jesus, you, as a redeemed believer, are called to sacrificial obedience.

This common calling unites us. Recognize the divine nature of it. God called us. We share a common experience of his grace.

A lot of things can divide Christians today (e.g., politics, preferences, programs), but we should always come back to this great, uniting reality: We have been called to Christ together, regardless of what our other differences may be, and our differences should never be viewed as being more important than our calling to Christ.

United by Christlike Conduct (4:2-3)

Paul now explains what it looks like to "walk worthy." In short, it looks like Jesus! Paul mentions the following character qualities that we must pursue as Christians: "with all humility and gentleness, with patience, bearing with one another in love, making every effort to keep the unity of the Spirit through the bond of peace" (Eph. 4:2-3).

Jesus was the supreme example of humility (Phil. 2:5-11). As for gentleness, Jesus said, "Come to Me . . . because I am gentle" (Matt. 11:28-29, ESV). His patience is unparalleled (1 Tim. 1:16). As for love, Christ demonstrated it in manifold ways, and most vividly at the cross (Rom. 5:8). As for being eager to maintain peace, he was the Peacemaker (Eph. 2:14). Therefore, the more we look like Jesus individually the more united we will become corporately.

Humility. Paul holds up humility throughout his letters as an essential characteristic of believers. He also speaks of humility in relation to unity (Rom. 12:3-8, Phil. 2:1-11; Col. 3:12-15). For unity to exist, there must be humble, selfless people, living for the good of others.

Gentleness. This does not mean timidity. It involves being "mild-spirited" or "self-controlled." Moses was described as the meekest man on the face of the earth (Num. 12:3). Yet he was a dynamic leader who challenged the power of the throne of Egypt. His strength stood under God's control (albeit imperfectly). Gentleness is a fruit of the Spirit, and it is the way we are to care for one another (Gal. 5:23; 6:1).

Patience. How are you doing with this virtue? For some of us, the microwave is too slow! "O Lord, give me patience, and hurry!" is our prayer. Paul reminds us that "Love is patient" (1 Cor. 13:4). To have patient love, we must endure annoyances and challenges over a period of time. How do you cultivate patience? By relying on the Spirit! And by meditating on the patience that Christ has shown you (cf. 1 Tim. 1:15-16; 2 Pet. 3:9). It is easy to learn facts; it is hard to be patient with people.

Bearing with one another in love. This basically means to "put up with each other in love." Peter says, "Love covers a multitude of sins" (1 Pet. 4:8). This is the only way relationships work. There are some difficult people in Christ's church, and you are likely that person from time to time! Paul sketches out similar characteristics needed for such unity in Colossians 3:12-15, including this call to bear with one another. It is a timeless and timely word for every local church.

Making every effort to keep the unity of the Spirit through the bond of peace. Unity is active, not passive. We should be zealous to maintain unity. Notice we do not work to create unity, but to keep unity! God alone creates our unity through Christ, but we are to maintain unity by the Spirit's help.

In order to pursue these qualities, we must be willing to renounce the opposite of each. We must renounce self-centeredness in order to walk in humility. We must renounce harshness in order to walk with gentleness. We must renounce the tyranny of our own agendas in order to walk with patience. We must renounce idealistic expectations in order to walk in forbearing love. We must renounce indifference and passivity in order to be eager to maintain the unity of the Spirit in the bond of peace. The church is unified and God is glorified when we live with such Christlike conduct.

United by Gospel Confession (4:4-6)

Paul cites what was probably an early Christian creed. The apostle points out seven "one" statements to emphasize the oneness we share in the gospel. It is important to note that Ephesians 4 is not teaching unity at any cost. It is a unity in Christ.

One body. We share a common existence in Christ's church. We are diverse in background and gifting, but we are united as one.

One Spirit. We share a common origin in the Holy Spirit's work. The Spirit is the One who creates unity and empowers us to maintain it.

One hope. We share a common hope in Christ. Formerly, we were "without hope" (Eph. 2:12) until we were called to Christ. Now we have hope, and we must live in a manner worthy of our calling.

One Lord. When the early Christians said, "Jesus is Lord," they were saying, "Caesar is not lord." When a Jewish Christian said this, they were boldly identifying Jesus with the God of the Jewish Scriptures (cf. Deut. 6:4). So this was not merely an empty creedal affirmation for early believers. This confession could cause you to lose your head.

One faith. The creed reminds us that we embrace the essential truths together, for "faith" here seems to refer to the body of truth we believe.

One baptism. We share a common experience of being spiritually baptized into Christ. We are united with Him. The act of baptism into water pictures this reality.

One God and Father. As His adopted children, we share the same Father (cf. Eph. 1:5). He is the God over all but is the Father of all His children—regardless of their ethnicity. We are one big, adopted family.

Notice also the Trinity here in this creed. The triune God not only creates the unity we have as believers but also serves as the ultimate picture of unity. Jesus prayed for unity, reflecting on His relationship with the Father (John 17:21). A healthy church is characterized by such unity, and it is a marvelous testimony to the watching world.

A Healthy Church Is Marked by Spiritual Diversity
EPHESIANS 4:7-12

Unity does not mean sameness. Our diverse roles and abilities enrich and bless the church. Paul shows us how the church, with all its glorious diversity, functions in a healthy way.

We Have Diverse Gifts (4:7-10)

Notice that every believer has received a gift, or "grace" (Eph. 4:7; cf. Rom. 12:4-8; 1 Cor. 12-14). This is not "saving grace" but "ministry grace." It is grace that is given to every believer to do ministry.

Perhaps what is most distinctive about this text, compared to the other texts on gifts, is the exalted, Christ-centered focus of it. Paul highlights Christ's generosity and Christ's authority. Christ Jesus died, rose, and ascended into heaven as the victorious King with all authority and gave gifts to His people, displaying extravagant generosity (Eph. 4:8).

These gifts are ways in which we extend the ministry of Jesus on this earth. When you see gifts at work, you should adore Jesus who gave them. When someone's gifts bless you, you should see that as Jesus blessing you.

In verse 8 Paul cites Psalm 68 and relates it to Christ's triumph and authority. Instead of directly quoting Psalm 68:18, Paul gives a general summary of the entire Psalm. It is a victory hymn. Historically it was typical after a king won a significant military victory to bring back the spoils of war (cf. Num. 31:7-9; 2 Sam. 12:29-31; Ex. 3:19-22). Here, having triumphed over sin, death, hell, and the grave, our Savior gave His church spiritually gifted people that they might minister to His church.

In verses 9-10, which function like a parenthesis, Paul speaks of Christ's descent and ascent. Paul sees Christ's descent and ascent as evidence that Christ is Savior and King. Christ is now above all. Christ fills all. Christ gives gifts to all His people. Marvel at His generosity to His people and authority over all!

📖 SPIRITUAL GIFTS INVENTORY

Paul elaborates on the value of using spiritual gifts for the common good in the body of Christ in other books of the Bible in addition to Ephesians.

See some of the roles commonly held by members of the church and match each to the spiritual gift needed.

Roles	Gifts
Mentor/counselor	Mercy
Bible study leader	Faith
Prayer warrior	Service
Greeter	Wisdom
Benevolence	Hospitality
Church secretary	Teaching

We Have Diverse Responsibilities (4:11-12a)

Christ gave us gifts so that we would use them (see 1 Pet. 4:10-11). These responsibilities are different for different believers. Here, Paul notes the leaders and the members.

The leaders equip the saints (4:11). Paul mentions those in unique positions of leadership in the church: apostle, prophet, evangelist, pastor, and teacher. The focus is on those gifted in articulating the gospel, teaching the Word, and shepherding God's people.

The titles **apostle** and **prophet** have a broad range. In one sense, the apostles and prophets were foundational to the church (Eph. 2:20; 3:5). *Apostle*, in a technical sense, refers to the Twelve (defined in this way, we do not have apostles anymore). In a general sense it can refer to a "sent one." Prophets were forth-tellers even more than future-tellers. We see prophets throughout the Old Testament but also mentioned in the early church in the New Testament (Acts 11:27-28; 13:1; 15:32; 21:9; 1 Cor. 14:32). In a general sense, prophets are those who apply God's Word to God's people.

Evangelists are those gifted in proclaiming the gospel (Acts 21:8; 2 Tim. 4:5). Everyone is called to evangelize, but some are uniquely gifted in this area.

The term **pastor** is used here to refer to a ministry in the church, though the related verb *shepherd* appears elsewhere (e.g., 1 Pet. 5:2; Acts 20:28; John 21:16). *Pastor* is to be understood alongside the terms *elder* and *overseer* (cf. Acts 14:23; 20:17,28; 1 Tim. 4:14; 5:17,19; Titus 1:5,7; 1 Pet. 5:1-4). In addition to the important role of teaching, pastors are to oversee the flock (1 Thess. 5:12; Heb. 13:17). They nurture, defend, protect, know, and sacrifice for the flock.

Some take teacher as the same office as pastors, translating them "pastor-teacher." There is clearly a close connection between the two (cf. Gal. 6:6; 1 Tim. 3:2; Titus 1:9).

While one may wrestle with these distinctive positions and gifts, one thing is abundantly clear: God has blessed His people throughout redemptive history with gifted proclaimers of His Word. Such leaders are instruments in the Redeemer's hands, used for our sanctification. Their teaching strengthens us and, as Paul says next, equips us for ministry.

The saints do the work of ministry (4:12). Church leaders prepare, complete, train, and equip God's people for ministry. We all have a work of ministry because we all have spiritual gifts given to us by Christ (1 Cor. 12:7,11; 1 Pet. 4:10). The pastors work and the people work. The church is to have an "every-member ministry."

What are you doing with what God has given you? The church will be enriched in worship and mission when everyone is serving. When members give, work in childcare, visit those in need, make meals for new parents, and minister to one another in groups, the body is edified, blessed, and built up (Eph. 4:12).

A Healthy Church Is Marked by Spiritual Maturity
EPHESIANS 4:13-16

The result of the church's unity and diversity is the church's maturity. Notice how this body metaphor in verse 13, "maturity," is contrasted with "children" in verse 14. Paul wants the people to grow up. Notice also that while one

 **COMPLETENESS**

While oneness is the focus of the session passage, did you notice another significant and fascinating number that shows up often throughout the Scriptures? Seven is the number associated with completeness in the Bible.

See the examples below for deeper insight and just a hint at the mathematical marvel the Bible contains:

Genesis 1 describes the seven _____ of creation.

Jesus gave seven "I am" statements recorded in John: the _____ of life (John 6:35); the _____ of the world (John 8:12); the _____ to salvation (John 10:9); the good _____ (John 10:11); the _____ and the life (John 11:25-26); the way, the _____, and the Life (John 14:6); and the _____ (John 15:5).

Jesus uttered seven statements on the cross as recorded in the gospels: 1) Father, _____ them, because they do not know what they are doing (Luke 23:34); Today you will be with me in _____ (Luke 23:43); 3) Woman, here is your _____. Here is your _____ (John 19:26-27); 4) My God, my God, why have you _____ me? (Mark 15:34); 5) I'm _____ (John 19:28); 6) It is _____ (John 19:30); 7) Father, into your hands I entrust my _____ (Luke 23:46).

is doing the work of ministry (Eph. 4:12), he or she grows into maturity. We tend to think that one must be totally mature to serve in the church, and while we must be careful not to appoint leaders too quickly, we need to recognize that spiritual growth is not merely cerebral. Service is a means of growth in maturity. Paul mentions four traits of a spiritually mature person.

Maturity Involves Christlikeness (4:13)

The ultimate picture of maturity is Christ—"A stature measured by Christ's fullness" (Eph. 4:13). "Christ's fullness" is an expression of completion or perfection. This makes obvious sense. The goal for us is to be like Jesus. We should long for the character qualities Paul mentioned in verses 2-3 to be present in our lives. We should long for maturity individually and corporately.

Maturity Involves Doctrinal Stability (4:13-14)

Paul mentions the need to grow in our "knowledge" of truth. In verse 13 he mentions growth in "unity in the faith" and "the knowledge of God's Son." In verse 14, he says that we should no longer be "little children" thrown around by every wind of doctrine.

Children are gullible and easily deceived. False teachers can creep in and toss them around. Children must be taught as they grow up. You would not say to your nine-year-old daughter, "Hey sweetheart, will you drive your brothers and sisters to corporate worship?" She is only nine years old! She has to be taught. And so do believers. We enter the Christian life as babies, but we are to grow through the Word and become disciple-making teachers (cf. 1 Pet. 2:1-3; Heb. 5:11-14).

Maturity Involves Truth Joined with Love (4:15-16)

God means for Christians to present the truth to others, and it should always be presented in love. We must hold the truth high (1 Tim. 3:15). And Christians must remember the centrality of love (1 Cor. 13).

The wording in Greek in verse 15 is "truthing in love."[2] Of course, "truthing" is not a word in English, but the idea is clear. Maturity involves a truth-telling, truth-maintaining, truth-doing love. Are you known for truth and love personally, and is your church known for truth and love corporately?

Maturity Involves Contribution (4:16)

Paul returns to the body metaphor, where every member is a part of Christ's body. Because you are a body part, you are important! We need each other. Every member is to contribute, using what he or she has.

Our ultimate need is Christ. We grow up into Him (Eph. 4:15). We are dependent on Christ, who is the head and source of the church. But we are also members of the body, and we are dependent on each other. "[E]ach part . . . working properly, makes the body grow so that it builds itself up in love" (4:16 ESV). As we grow into Christ, and as we use our gifts—in love—the body becomes healthy. What an unspeakable privilege it is to be united to Christ and to one another!

It is wise and good to be health conscious—taking care of our physical bodies. But let us be more concerned about the health of the body of Christ. May our local church bodies be marked by spiritual unity, spiritual diversity, and an ever-increasing maturity. Paul's teaching serves as a "spiritual checkup" in these vital areas. Let us make the necessary changes by the Spirit's help.

A CLOSER LOOK

Humility

Interestingly, the term "humility" was uncommon in first-century Greek literature, and when it does appear, it is used with a negative connotation.[3] Pride was more highly valued. Christians were ridiculed for humility.[4] However, this virtue is valued throughout the Old Testament Scriptures (Prov. 3:34; 11:2; Isa. 66:2), and perfectly displayed in Jesus (Phil. 2:5-11).

We live in a similar day. This is a day of "selfies" and "self-exaltation," not the day of humble servants. To pursue such a life requires the Spirit's power and our willingness to put to death our ego and selfish ambition.

Paul describes humility in Philippians 2:3 within the context of considering others more important than ourselves. He does not describe humility as "self-loathing." Rather, it is about thinking about the well-being of others. Tim Keller puts it this way: "The essence of gospel-humility is not thinking more of myself or thinking less of myself, it is thinking of myself less."[5] This others-oriented focus is at the heart of being a servant of Christ.

It may come as a surprise to some that this kind of humble, Christ-centered, others-oriented life is freeing and fulfilling! That is because a self-absorbed life is a miserable life. And not only is a life of humble service satisfying, but it serves as the great means to unity in the church.

PERSONAL REFLECTION

1. Why is unity important in a local church?

2. What do all believers share in common? What should all believers be pursuing?

3. Explain the relationship between leaders in a local church and members of a local church.

4. Which of the marks of spiritual maturity (vv. 13-16) stuck out to you the most? Why?

1. Klyne Snodgrass, *Ephesians*. The NIV Application Commentary (Grand Rapids: Zondervan, 1996), 218.
2. John R. W. Stott, *God's New Society: The Message of Ephesians,* The Bible Speaks Today (Downers Grove, IL: InterVarsity Press, 1979)172.
3. Thielman, *Ephesians*. Baker Exegetical Commentary on the New Testament (Grand Rapids: Baker, 2010), 253.
4. Thielman, *Ephesians*, 253.
5. Timothy Keller, *The Freedom of Self Forgetfulness: The Path to Christian Joy*. Lancashire, UK: 10 Publishing, 2012. Kindle.

WE ARE MADE NEW

EPHESIANS 4:17–6:9

I recall hearing a story about the North African church father, Augustine, that has stuck with me. Whether historically accurate or not, it illustrates a powerful truth. After his dramatic conversion, he reportedly encountered one of his many girlfriends, who began chasing him down the street declaring, "Augustine, Augustine, it is I; It is I." (His pre-Christian life was characterized by lust and sexual sin, as he confessed). But Augustine kept running away. She persisted. Eventually, this newly converted man, soon to become the great theologian, stated, "But it is not I; it is not I; it is not I." That is what happens when you experience new life in Christ. You get a new identity. And consequently, everything changes.

Paul now shows us how our new identity in Christ leads to new ethical commitments and new relational perspectives and practices. Notice three ways Jesus changes everything: (1) the new self, (2) a new walk, and (3) new relationships.

The New Self
EPHESIANS 4:17-32

Formerly but Now (4:17-24)

Paul reminds the Ephesians that prior to Christ's salvation, they (like we) were cut off from spiritual life. Their hearts were hardened, and their desire for sin expressed itself in manifold ways (Eph. 4:17-19). But then he explains why they must not live as pagans. Short answer: they are new in Christ!

Paul says, "you came to know Christ" (4:20). Christianity is about knowing a living person, Jesus Christ. Further, we "were taught by him" (4:21). All ethical instructions are to be understood in light of our union with Christ.

Finally, we see that Christ is the truth. Paul declares "the truth is in Jesus" (4:21c). The truth is not just a set of propositions. The truth has fingernails, and scarred hands; it is in a person: Jesus (John 14:6).

The apostle goes on to urge the Ephesians to "take off your former way of life" (Eph. 4:22). Do not go back to it! Remember that you do not wear this old garment any longer!

In verse 23, Paul says that new self involves a life of renewal: "To be renewed in the spirit of your minds" (cf. Col. 3:10). "Being renewed" is in the present tense, indicating that this renewal is an ongoing process that God performs in us.

In verse 24 the "new self" refers to our new identity in Christ. When we put on Christ, we say with Augustine, "It is not I."

The good news in this passage is that God can transform anyone by His grace. Many in the Ephesian church matched this dark description, but they became new creations.

The point is clear: as new creations in Christ, we are to think differently, respond to the truth differently, and act differently than the pagan culture. God enables us to live holy lives by His Holy Spirit (cf. Eph. 4:29; 5:18). To be clear, it is not that you should never be around unbelievers. You should! But like Jesus, the goal is to be separate from sin, even though we must not be isolated from unbelievers.

Living Out This New Identity (4:25-32)

The following five exhortations are not an exhaustive list of examples on how to live out our new identity, but they are vitally important and should mark our lives:

1. Replace lying with truth-telling (Eph. 4:25)
2. Replace unrighteous anger with righteous anger (4:26-27)
3. Replace stealing with working and giving (4:28)
4. Replace corrupt talk with edifying talk (4:29-30)
5. Replace bitterness and rage with kindness and forgiveness (4:31-32)

Notice, these practical exhortations are **relational.** Our new union with Christ should change the way we live in **community.**

Further, observe how there is a **negative** action stated first and then a **positive** action. Holiness is not just about saying "no" to sin; it is also about saying "yes" to God. We must not just throw our dirty clothes in the hamper; we must put on the new suit as well!

Finally, consider that there are **theological reasons** given for why you should throw off these sinful vices and put on these Christian actions. Paul does not simply say, "Put away lying"; he relates it to ecclesiology: "Because we are members of one another" (4:25). He does not stop with the exhortation, "Be angry and do not sin" (4:26); he relates it to a belief in the "devil" (4:27). He commands the church to no longer "steal" and follows it by speaking of honest work and stewardship (4:28). When talking about unhealthy speech, he relates it to grieving the Holy Spirit (4:29-30). Regarding forgiveness, he takes us to the cross and God's amazing forgiveness (4:31-32). Our practice and our theology are tied together. Christians should not only live differently than unbelievers, but they should do so **for different reasons.**

A New Walk
EPHESIANS 5:1-17

In Ephesians 5:1-17, Paul goes on to describes how our new identity in Christ comes with the calling to imitate God (5:1) by walking in love, light, and wisdom (5:2-17).

Walk in Love (5:2)

Paul goes back to the cross of Christ in verse 2 to talk about love. How did Jesus love? This verse provides a marvelous description of genuine love. Love involves giving ourselves away for the good of another. Jesus "loved us and gave himself for us" (Eph. 5:2).

Paul adds that Christ's death was a "sacrificial and fragrant offering to God" (5:2). Christ gave Himself up for us, but it was an offering to God. This is the pattern of love for us. We are to love sacrificially for the glory of God.

Walk in Light (5:3-14)

Paul mentions several sins here to describe a dark life: sexual immorality, impurity, greed, and filthy speech (Eph. 5:3-5). These sins grow out of a heart that has replaced God with functional saviors. One might think we are advanced in the twenty-first century. But when you read this list of sins, you see that we have the same sin issues today.

Sexual immorality is at the top of Paul's sin lists elsewhere (Col. 3:5; cf. Gal. 5:19; 1 Cor. 6:9-11). The word used here for sexual immorality is *pornei*, a broad term applicable to various sexual sins (eg., fornication, adultery, bestiality) and also lustful thoughts (Matt. 5:27-30).

Ultimately, *pornei* is idolatry. Much of the ancient world had sexual practices wrapped up in their idolatry (as in Ephesus). Paul shows us this progression in Romans 1:18-32. Your life is an overflow of your heart. Your sexual sin problem is fundamentally a worship problem. Paul's words are timely and timeless.

Greed (or covetousness) is the insatiable desire for more. Paul identifies it as idolatry in verse 5 and in Colossians 3:5 (cf. Ex. 20:4). Greed is about desiring something more than God. Jesus told his followers to "watch out and be on guard against all greed" and not to become a rich fool (Luke 12:15-21). Greed is sneaky. I heard Tim Keller once say in all his years of pastoring, no one every confessed the sin of greed to him! Why? Because no one thinks they are greedy!

Corrupt speech (5:4). Christians must also avoid "coarse and foolish talking or crude joking." Those walking in the light will not use language that is shameful or disgraceful (cf. Col. 3:8). And while there is nothing wrong with humor and laughter, humor can be abused in malicious and vulgar ways. Therefore, Paul forbids "crude joking."

Paul says that in place of corrupt speech, the Christian should be known for "giving thanks" (Eph. 5:4). Sexual sin, greed, and corrupt talk are about self-centered ways of thinking. But thanksgiving is a God-centered way of thinking.

Warning (5:5-6). Those who persist in this dark lifestyle will not inherit the kingdom of heaven. Christians will sin in these ways from time to time, but not in habitual, unrepentant sin. Paul strengthens his argument by speaking of the fate of the unrepentant. He says God's wrath is coming on the unrepentant (5:6).

Exhibit the Fruit of Light (5:7-10). Paul reminds us of our new identity and gives us four instructions on how we can exhibit the fruit of light amidst darkness.

- Display light by not joining those in darkness. (5:7).
- Display light by living out your identity as those who are "light in the Lord" (5:8).
- Display light by doing all that is good, right, and true (5:9).
- Display light by pleasing the Lord (5:10).

OLD SELF/NEW LIFE

If you are in Christ, your life has experienced marked changes with striking contrasts between before and after. Fill in the chart below to illustrate some differences in your own life. The last lines are left blank to add items personal to you. If there are areas where you have not experienced much change, what would you say is holding you back?

	Old Self	New Life
Thought life		
Interest in prayer/Bible/church		
Anger		
Speech		
Work ethic		
Bad habits		
Relationships		
_____		
_____		
_____		

In other words, be who you are! You are light, now live in a way that is consistent with that new identity.

Expose the Darkness (5:11-14). Believers must not only avoid participation in darkness, but they must also actively expose the darkness. Walking in the light does not mean avoiding contact with people. It means to live a holy life, and it means confronting darkness.

We need wisdom, discernment, gentleness, and courage to know how to confront and expose the works of darkness. Paul says that the light illuminates darkness, as evil is seen for what it is.

Further, Paul says that light transforms unbelievers into the realm of light (5:14). There is a transforming power of the light of truth and purity. J. B. Philips' paraphrase is helpful: "It is even possible [after all, it happened to you!] for the light to turn the thing it shines upon into light also" (5:14). We must bring the light of justice, exposing shameful, secretive sins, and bring the transforming light of the gospel to everyone, including the guilty enslavers themselves.

The last part of verse 14 is about the transforming light of Christ. These words are probably a hymn or an early confession, used at baptism. Paul says, "Get up, sleeper, and rise up from the dead, and Christ will shine on you" (5:14).

Walk in Wisdom (5:15-17)

The believer's new walk is also marked by wisdom: "pay careful attention, then, to how you walk—not as unwise people but as wise" (Eph. 5:15). Paul gives some specific ways to do this in verses 16-17.

Making the Most of the Time (5:16). Christians should make the most of their time because they do not want to waste their lives. The phrase "the days are evil" refers to the idea of this "present evil age" (Gal. 1:4) in which we all are living. We must passionately shine our light in this dark world while we have breath.

Understand What the Lord's Will Is (5:17). Usually when Christians talk about God's will, they are referring to God's will regarding major decisions about things like their career. But I do not think that is what Paul has in mind here. He is referring to God's already revealed will, and for us today, that means understanding the Bible. The wise prayerfully apply God's word to specific situations so that they can honor the Lord in all things.

New Relationships
EPHESIANS 5:18-6:9

One of the most important results of our new life is that we have new relationships. Because of the gospel, we view our relationships differently than the unbelieving world.

Be Filled with the Spirit (5:18-21)

Here is the fountain of healthy relationships: the Holy Spirit.

Paul gives a few evidences of the Spirit: singing joyfully as a community to the Lord (Eph. 5:19) and giving thanks to God (5:20). He adds, "submitting to one another in the fear of Christ" (5:21). The word *submit* means "to arrange under." It was used in the military to refer to the subordination of soldiers. The motive: "in the fear of Christ" or out of reverence for Christ. We submit to others because Christ is the ultimate authority over our lives.

Husbands and Wives (5:22-33)

Paul begins with wives (Eph. 5:22-24). While many struggle with the idea of wives "submitting," remember that the wife is called to submit to a husband that is dying for her! The husband should be the first to apologize, forgive, and serve. He is to exemplify the lifestyle of Jesus to his bride.

Paul goes on to say later that the wife must also show "respect" for her husband (5:33). On a practical level, the husband needs the wife's respect. The wife should see the responsibility that he has and respect him, love him, pray for him, and respect his needs.

We must reject all improper caricatures of this teaching. Scripture is not talking about something akin to slavery, subservience, nor of a top-down chain of command, where the subjects have to obey without question.

Paul says that the motive of godly, loving submission is this: "As to the Lord" (5:22). Wives submit to their husbands because they want to glorify Christ. The godly wife sees this duty as part of her Christian discipleship. The motive is not to fulfill some societal role or some cultural expectation. The motive is love for Christ and a desire to be conformed to His image.

Paul speaks of marriage as a **picture** of Christ's love for the church in verses 23-24, and carries it into verses 25-32. Paul shows us that marriage displays the gospel. In verse 32 Paul says this picture is "profound." Wives give a picture of the church to the world (5:24). Husbands give a picture of Christ to the world (5:23). Christ is the head, as noted in 1:22. But look what kind of head He is. Peek into the next paragraph and consider the six actions of His leadership:

1. He loved the church (5:25)
2. He gave Himself up for her (5:25)
3. He sanctified her (5:26)
4. He cleansed her (5:26)
5. He presented her (5:27)
6. He "provides and cares for" the church (5:29)

Additionally, this illustration gives us the ultimate **purpose** of marriage: the glory of Christ. Everything in this passage points us to Christ: "As to the Lord" (5:22); "as Christ loved the church" (5:25); "as Christ does for the church" (5:29).

📖 REPLACEMENT PARTS

One of the ways we get rid of persistent bad behaviors is to replace them with good ones. Consider the list below and decide what you can do instead to turn a negative into a positive. The first two are done for you.

Anger: Take a walk to cool down when you lose your cool.

Gossip: Make a habit of saying a positive aloud every time you hear a negative about someone.

Lust:

Envy:

Greed:

Unforgiveness:

Hate:

While it is important for couples to work through communication problems, financial problems, personality issues, the past, and other issues, let us remember that the ultimate issue in marriage is this: Are you surrendered to the Lordship of Christ? Will you submit to Him in all areas of life?

Finally, this illustration provides amazing **hope** for marriage. Christ died for the church, which displayed her sinfulness and His saving grace. The biggest problem in marriage is sin. The ultimate solution is the grace of Jesus. Where do you look when marriage is difficult? Look to Christ. Marriage is intended to point us to our Redeemer.

Parents and Children (6:1-4)

Next, Paul provides instructions for the Christian household, covering matters of honor and discipleship.

Children can honor their parents through a proper attitude. They should listen, learn, and follow their parents in a spirit of respect, as unto the Lord.

Further, children are called to obey their parents by hearing and doing what their parents say (see Col. 3:20). Children will have a hard time obeying their parents. When they do not obey, they need to be reminded that Jesus died for disobedient sinners. Parents can make disobedience an occasion to teach the gospel.

Why should a child obey his or her parents? Paul says, "Because it is right" (Eph. 6:1). And adds the promise of both blessing: "That it may go well with you," and safekeeping: "That you may have long life in the land." Paul combines Exodus 20:12 and Deuteronomy 5:16. The original promise to Israel involved a long and good life in the land of Israel. Paul omits the focus on Israel and makes the statement more general and proverbial.

The word translated "Fathers" (6:4) is a word that is actually used in Hebrews 11:23 to refer to both parents. Paul could have both parents in mind, but more likely he is turning attention to fathers. Practically, both parents need to teach the kids. Paul told Timothy to hold fast to the instruction he received from his mother and grandmother (2 Tim. 1:5; 3:14). Timothy seems to have had an unbelieving dad; fortunately, his mothers taught him.

Parents must work hard to not to "stir up anger" in their children, and to bring them up in the "training and instruction of the Lord" (6:4). This requires consistency and discipline on the part of parents who are empowered by the Spirit.

Slaves and Masters (6:5-9)

Finally, Paul gives instructions to slaves and masters, exhorting them to glorify Christ with proper attitudes, work ethic, and a deep awareness of Christ's lordship.

The context here is not like slavery in American history. The slavery of Paul's day was complex and massive in scope. American slavery was primarily racial and lifelong. In Paul's day, it was not racial and it was not always lifelong. There were some similarities, but it was very different. Some estimate that a third of the population in the city of Ephesus were slaves, so this was an important relationship to address.

Paul's goal here is not to write a document about changing the institution of slavery. It was to instruct Christians how to glorify God in their existing situation. Paul does not condone slavery. (The New Testament teaches that human trafficking/slave trading is a sin; see 1 Tim. 1:10). Paul is simply giving instructions as to how to live within the cultural situation. And it should be noted that many have pointed out that slavery slowly died out in antiquity due to the influence of Christianity. Paul describes the ethics required between Christian slaves and Christian masters, thereby changing typical relationships between master and slave. By changing how they related to one another, he essentially planted the seeds for the destruction of this system.

How does Paul tell slave and master to relate to each other? First, he admonishes both slave and master to treat each other as they would Christ. Notice in each verse, either "Christ," "Master," or "Lord" are mentioned.

Second, Paul reminds both slave and master that they are under the lordship of Christ, and "there is no favoritism with Him" (Eph. 6:9).

Third, Paul calls masters to show justice and reciprocity toward slaves. This idea was nowhere to be found in the legal code in Paul's day. Yet Paul says so here in Ephesians: "Masters, treat your slaves the same way, without threatening them" (6:9).

Paul considers the existing structure and provides some gospel-centered instruction to both slaves and masters. He tells slaves do their work unto Christ, by working respectfully (6:5), wholeheartedly (6:5b-6), willingly (6:7), and expectantly (6:8). He tells masters to treat their slaves as they would treat Christ (6:9), which involved practicing mutuality, avoiding hostility, and living with a Christ-centered accountability (6:9).

This passage should change the way we work. Think about employees and employers. Can we make this application? I think so. If these principles applied in a working environment of slave/master, how much more should we seek to live them out in better working conditions? Here are some take-aways:

Employees: Work through Christ, like Christ, and for Christ.

Employer: Lead through Christ, like Christ, and for Christ.

Do your work through the power of Christ, reflecting the character of Christ, and to the glory of Christ.

A CLOSER LOOK

Marriage

The foundation for marriage is crumbling all around us. People are confused about gender, marriage, and family. Some are outright hostile to the historic Christian view on marriage. This is not simply a cultural war; it is a spiritual war. The enemy would love to confuse people and tear down the foundations of God's plan for marriage.

What is the biblical idea of marriage? Stott summarizes it well: "Marriage is an exclusive heterosexual covenant between one man and one woman, ordained and sealed by God, preceded by the leaving of parents, consummated in sexual union, issuing in a permanent mutually supportive partnership, and normally crowned with the gift of children."[1]

Let us affirm the goodness of marriage (and singleness, cf. 1 Cor. 7), and the covenant nature of marriage. It is intended to be permanent, sacred, intimate, mutual, and exclusive. Let us thank God for His beautiful design, and let us also be quick to minster God's grace to those who have had broken marriages. And let us remember that marriage in this life is a shadow of the ultimate marriage of Christ and His bride, as Paul illustrates in this text.

PERSONAL REFLECTION

1. What does it look like to "put off" the old self in order to embrace your new identity in Christ?

2. How are you challenged by the implications for earthly relationships Paul gives in light of the gospel?

3. How is marriage a picture of the gospel? If you are married, how does your marriage point others to the truth of the gospel?

4. How should your approach to your daily work change based on the exhortation Paul gives to slaves and masters?

1. John Stott, *Involvement: Social and Sexual Relationships in the Modern World*, Vol 2 (New Jersey: Revell, 1984), 163.

WE HAVE STRENGTH TO PERSEVERE

EPHESIANS 6:10-24

This passage on "the armor of God" is a favorite among Christians, and rightly so. We know that life is war, and we need God's power to overcome the temptations and trials of this life. But before we consider it closely, it is worth noting some important truths that are often missed.

First, this passage is rooted in the Old Testament. While Paul is certainly aware of Roman soldiers, and maybe even looking at them at the time of writing, his language is also (perhaps more) influenced by the majestic warfare imagery of the Old Testament, especially from Isaiah. The Old Testament often refers to God and His Messiah as a warrior and His people as "troops" who are in need of God's strength (see Ex. 15:3; Ps. 18:39; 35:1-3; Isa. 11:5; 42:13; 49:2; 52:7). Paul is picking up these allusions. This passage points us to the very nature of the Messiah and His mighty works. It is through our union with Christ, the triumphant Messiah, that we withstand the devil's schemes and attacks.

Second, this passage is a climactic conclusion to the whole book of Ephesians. The armor of God does not come out of nowhere. Paul alludes to several key ideas that were already mentioned in the letter:

- **Divine Power**—The call to "be strengthened by the Lord" (Eph. 6:10) draws our minds back to the earlier prayers (1:19-20; 3:16,20).
- **Already/Not Yet**—This passage reminds us that Christ has already triumphed over the powers of darkness (1:21; 3:10; 4:8), giving us new life and freeing us from the fear of these powers (2:2); but we have not yet experienced the full fruits of Christ's victory, for their powers still exist (though they are defeated!—4:27; 5:16). Ephesians 6 reminds us that a battle still rages.

- **Christlike Virtues**—The virtues connected with the pieces of armor have already been mentioned: truth (1:13; 4:15,21,24,25; 5:9), righteousness (4:24; 5:9), peace (2:14-18; 4:3), the gospel (1:13; 3:6), the Word of God (1:13; 5:26), salvation (1:13; 2:5,8; 5:23), and faith (1:13,15,19; 2:8; 3:12,17; 4:5,13).
- **Prayer**—The summons to prayer in 6:18-20 also reflects previous language like "all the saints" (3:18), "the mystery" (1:9; 3:3-4,9; 5:32), and "boldness" (3:12), as well as Paul's imprisonment (3:1; 4:1).
- **"Put on"**—Earlier Paul said that we should "put on the new self, created according to God's likeness" (4:24) and "be imitators of God" (5:1). Now, he says we should "put on the full armor of God" (6:11). The armor given to us is God's own armor. To put on the armor of God is to put on the Messiah Himself. It means to be identified with Him, and to fight with His strength, displaying His character.

Therefore, what we have here is a carefully put together conclusion that recaps and motivates the Christian.

Finally, this passage highlights the warfare involved in the relational and ethical challenges mentioned in Ephesians 4:1–6:9. As Stott says, "Beneath the surface, an unseen spiritual battle is raging."[1] We should not talk about relational and ethical problems apart from talking about spiritual warfare. We are in a broken world that is influenced by the "god of this age" (2 Cor. 4:4). We must consider the work of the enemy when trying to assess and solve the problems of this world. Paul is not uninformed about the real problems; he is informing us about the real, unseen battle beneath these visible problems, as a trustworthy and inspired apostle.

Stand Strong in Spiritual Warfare

In Ephesians 6:10-17 Paul exhorts the Ephesians (and us) to stand firm, by God's strength, in God's armor, in the midst of spiritual warfare. The three imperatives are "be strengthened," "put on the full armor of God," and "stand." These imperatives "dominate the text, the rest of the verses are explanatory."[2]

Notice also the repetition: "stand" (Eph. 6:11), "withstand" (6:13 ESV), "take your stand" (6:13), and "Stand, therefore" (6:14). In verse 14 "stand" is issued as an imperative, a central admonition in the text.

Further, observe a defensive element here. We must "resist" the devil's temptations (6:13; see also Jas. 4:7). Stand holding your ground, not giving in an inch. Say, "I will not yield to your temptation. I will not listen to your lies. I will not budge."

But there is also an offensive element in the text. We are to take up the sword of the Spirit (6:17) and speak the gospel in the face of opposition (6:19-20).

Paul also highlights a corporate element in the text. Together, we must put on the armor of God. We do not fight alone, but together with our fellow Christian warriors, who are reliant on God's power.

Be Aware of the Battle
EPHESIANS 6:10-13

We Need the Lord's Strength (6:10,11,13)

Paul begins with the charge to be strengthened by the Lord (Eph. 6:10). We must be strengthened by His mighty power because we do not want to crumble when the evil one tempts us.

Do not look in the wrong place for strength. Our strength is not in our resources and ability, in how long we have been Christians, in how much we know about the Bible, or how long we have been in ministry. Our strength is in our union with Jesus Christ and His mighty power (cf. 1:19).

We Need to Know Our Enemy (6:11-13)

Paul has already mentioned "the devil" in Ephesians (Eph. 4:27). His Greek title, *diabolos*, means "slanderer." He opposes. He accuses. *Satan* in Hebrew means "adversary." His various names in Scripture displays the fact that he is wicked, powerful, and cunning.

Consider how Paul describes the enemy here in Ephesians 6. He tells us that the devil is **evil**. He totally opposes God's ways and God's people. Paul mentions "the spiritual forces" of evil (6:12) and "the evil day" (6:13).

Further, the evil one is also **strategic.** In verse 11 Paul tells us to be aware of the devil's "schemes." Satan is wily, subtle, and devious. Satan can make sinful things look attractive and desirable, distorting the truth and camouflaging evil.

Inside the theater at Ephesus - looking up at the seats

ILLUSTRATOR PHOTO/TOM HOOKE

Next, the evil one **wrestles.** In verse 12 Paul says that we "struggle" or "wrestle" (ESV) not against flesh and blood but against spiritual forces of evil. It is a close, intense battle, filled with manipulation and strategy. The devil is not firing laser guided missiles from a distance; he is upon us (see Luke 22:31-32).

Some think that these "authorities" and "world powers" are political entities (Eph. 6:12). They think Paul is speaking about cultural and societal systems. Even though Satan surely can and does work through these systems, I do not think that is what Paul is referring to here. He seems to be speaking of the powers that work with the evil one in general.

We must also remember that the devil has been **defeated.** We can have confidence because Jesus has already won the victory for us (see 1:19-22; 4:8). We are not urged to win the battle here, but to stand firm. The authority of the powers has been broken, and their final defeat is coming soon. We are not called into this battle as if the victory is in doubt. The decisive victory has been won. We fight with confidence because all things will ultimately be put under Christ's feet!

In verse 13 Paul mentions "the evil day." In my view, this refers to the combination of the present evil age we are in (5:16) and of particularly tempting occasions. Consider Matthew 4:11 and the phrase "then the devil left Him." This presupposes that the devil had come in force on this occasion to tempt and destroy Jesus. While the evil one certainly wanted to

📖 PROFILES IN COURAGE

Engaging in spiritual battles requires courage above fear. See how courage made these role models famous and worth imitating.

After first refusing to intervene to help save my people, I listened to my cousin, reconsidered, and famously said, "If I perish, I perish" (Esther 4:16). Who am I? _____

I made excuses for why I shouldn't be the one to lead the Israelites out of captivity, until I finally stepped up to my calling and into my destiny (Exodus 6:28-7:7). Who am I? _____

I asked for a sign—and then another one—before God whittled down my army to a precious few. But who needs an army when God is on your side (Judges 6)? Who am I? _____

I agreed to go into battle on the condition that Deborah went with me. I found my courage, but the honor went to her, for good reason (Judges 4). Who am I? _____

Elijah called down fire from heaven, but I took my courage in my hands to serve him the last of the provisions I was saving for my starving son (1 Kings 17:7-16). Who am I? _____

attack Jesus all the time, there were still certain times when he came with particular force. We must stand against his schemes in our own days in which the battle is particularly intense.

Be Equipped with God's Armor
EPHESIANS 6:13-17

After telling us to put on the armor, Paul now describes it. The first thing to recognize is the armor is "of God" (Eph. 6:13). The same armor that the

Messiah wears in battle is also our battle gear. There is no reason to yield one inch to Satan if we have put on the full armor of God.

Belt of Truth (6:14a). As we buckle on this piece of the Messiah's armor, we live in His truth and speak His truth, displaying the characteristics of our victorious King. Do not give the devil a foothold by not being a person of truth—in your language, behavior, and attitude. Preach the truth of the gospel to yourself, and live in that truth throughout the day.

Breastplate of Righteousness (6:14b). For the Roman soldier, the breastplate covered the chest to protect it against assaults and arrows. Paul's language is drawn from Isaiah 59:17, where Yahweh puts on "righteousness as a breastplate" (ESV). Once again, we are to put on the virtues of our Messiah. Put on those righteous qualities associated with your new life in Christ, the righteous qualities reflected in the life of Jesus. Put on the breastplate of righteousness so that you do not give in an inch to Satan in the areas of impurity, lust, greed, or injustice. Realize who you are in Christ, and live out that new identity in righteous living.

Gospel Shoes (6:15). Paul says, "as shoes for your feet, having put on the readiness given by the gospel of peace" (6:15 ESV). Paul is basically saying believers should always be ready to herald the good news of Christ (cf. Isa. 52:7). Historians tell us that the Romans were issued great footwear. Their studded half boots enabled them to travel great distances. They covered a lot of ground in a short amount of time, pursuing the enemy into every nook and cranny. They went into hard places. We need to go to every nook and cranny also, proclaiming the "gospel of peace" (Eph. 6:15; see Isa 52:7). In the midst of this passage on warfare there is a message of peace. Through Christ, sinners can be reconciled with God and have peace (cf. Rom. 5:1).

Shield of Faith (6:16). The word Paul uses for "shield" is not the small one, the size of a Frisbee, that left the body exposed, but the big one, the size of a door, that covered the whole body. Biblical writers often refer to God as a shield (cf. Ps. 18:30; 28:7; Prov. 30:5). We have a shield to protect us from the darts of the enemy when we put on Christ, believing the promises of God. As we believe what he says about us, what he says is ours.

Helmet of Salvation (6:17a). Roman helmets were made of tough iron or bronze, with cheek guards, and with an inside lining of sponge that made the weight bearable.[3] Nothing short of an ax could penetrate these helmets. God's people are to put on the hope they have in Christ. If you are trusting in Christ, then do not listen to the devil's lies. Say to the evil one,

"I have been saved from sin's penalty, I am being saved from sin's power, and I will one day be saved from sin's presence." Put your helmet on, and do not let the evil one get to your head (cf. Isa. 59:17; 1 Thess. 5:8).

Sword of the Spirit (6:17a). The final piece of equipment is an offensive weapon. The believer must take up the sword and engage the enemy. Do not go into battle without a weapon! The term refers to a short sword or dagger, used in personal combat. Because this is a sword "of the Spirit," it is spiritually powerful in combat. Paul identifies it with God's Word. However, Paul normally uses *logos*, but here he uses *rhema*, which usually refers to the spoken word. If that is the case here, then he is referring to speaking the gospel in the midst of the war. Again, one hears echoes from Isaiah here about the Messiah (Isa 11:4; 49:2; cf. Rev. 19:15). We are given access to the weaponry of the Messiah for battle when we are united with Him. We are to speak the gospel in the realm of darkness so that those who are held captive by the evil one may go free.

Be Devoted to Prayer
EPHESIANS 6:18-20

Paul does not begin a new sentence in verse 18. It is a continuation of thought. We stand firm against the enemy's schemes through **prayer.** We are to take up the sword of the Spirit prayerfully.

Unlike the other items previously mentioned, prayer is not associated with a piece of armor or equipment. However, a modern piece of equipment does comes to mind: a walkie-talkie. John Piper uses this picture in describing prayer:

> We cannot know what prayer is for until we know that life is war. Life is war. That's not all it is. But it is certainly that. Our weakness in prayer is owing largely to our neglect of this truth. Prayer is primarily a wartime walkie-talkie for the mission of the church as it advances against the powers of darkness and unbelief. It is not surprising that prayer malfunctions when we try to make it a domestic intercom to call upstairs for more comforts in the den. God has given us prayer as a wartime walkie-talkie so that we can call headquarters for everything we need as the kingdom of Christ advances in the world.[4]

📖 ONE HOPEFUL STEP AT A TIME

Characters in the Bible engaged in spiritual battle. Which pieces of the armor did they use? Add the letters below.

a.Truth   b. Gospel of Peace   c. Righteousness   d. Faith   e. the Word
f. Salvation   g. Spirit

_____ Job through all his tribulations (Job 13:15)

_____ Daniel in the lion's den (Dan. 6)

_____ Jesus and Peter at Jesus's arrest (John 18:1-12)

_____ Jesus before Pilate (John 18:36)

_____ Jesus when He was tempted (Luke 4:1-13)

_____ Stephen as he was martyred (Acts 7:54-59)

_____ An imprisoned Paul before he died (2 Tim. 1:12)

While such a device is not in Paul's mind, Piper's illustration reminds us of Paul's point, that it is through prayer that we communicate with our God and ask for his help.

When Paul says, "Pray at all times in the Spirit" (Eph. 6:18) I do not think he is referring to "speaking in tongues." We should understand Paul's words in light of the rest of Ephesians. We should simply take it as a fact that all true prayer is by the Spirit. Because of the gift of the Spirit, the Christian warrior has constant access to God when the battle rages.

Pray Comprehensively (6:18)

Paul mentions four universals (four "alls") to express the comprehensiveness of prayer. We pray "**at all times**." So everywhere, all the time, we can pray.

We pray "**with all prayer and supplication**" (ESV). I doubt a sharp distinction is intended here with these two words. Paul is simply emphasizing faithful prayer.

We should stay alert with "**with all perseverance.**" Like good soldiers, we need to keep alert and not fall asleep. This idea appeared in the ministry of Jesus, who encouraged His disciples to "stay awake and pray" in light of temptation and the weakness of the flesh (Mark 14:38) and in view of the return of Christ (Mark 13:32-38; cf. 1 Pet. 4:7). We read about persistence and perseverance in prayer elsewhere in the New Testament (Acts 2:42; 4:23-31; 6:4; 12:5; Rom. 12:12, Col. 4:2). We need to persist in prayer to overcome fatigue, discouragement, and hardship, and for boldness in our witness.

The last "all" is making intercession "**for all the saints.**" The unity of the church has been a major concern in the letter. Now, Paul says that we should pray for all other Christians. When you become a Christian you get a new family, which means a new responsibility to pray for them.

The focus on "all" emphasizes the fact that because all of life is war, all of life must be lived in prayer. Since there is a war, pray. Pray all the time. Pray with all prayer and supplication. Pray alertly and persistently. Pray for all the saints.

Pray for Gospel Boldness (6:19-20)

Paul, the prisoner in chains, humbly requests prayer from others because he wants to boldly and effectively communicate the good news. The greatest theologian-missionary of all time is asking for prayer! That should encourage you! He has the position (as do we) of being an "ambassador," a representative of Jesus, but he knows that he does not have sufficient resources to communicate the gospel effectively, so he calls on the church to pray for him. Instead of feeling self-pity or resentment, he asks for prayer for the mission!

Pray for others as they share the gospel. Why? Satan does not want us to have the right words to say or to be bold in the face of conflict. Evangelism is spiritual warfare. The culture opposes it. So we need God's power to do it faithfully.

Final Remarks
EPHESIANS 6:21-24

After speaking of his need for God's power to speak the Word and of his imprisonment, Paul closes with a reminder about his particular situation. Here we see that Paul was not just a theologian-missionary-church planter. He was a lover of people. In his letters, he thanks people.

Tychicus is one of the brothers that made up the family of God. He served with Paul for some time (Acts 20:4; Col. 4:7; 2 Tim. 4:12; Titus 3:12). Tychicus may have delivered the letter to Ephesus (and the letter to the Colossians). Can you imagine that task?

Paul sends him to "encourage your hearts" (Eph. 6:22). What a great ministry! In many ways, Tychicus does what every missionary-preacher-evangelist does. He spreads the Word and encourages the saints.

In the benediction (6:23-24) Paul concludes by using the words with which he began his letter: peace and grace (cf. 1:2). He also mentions faith and love. It is appropriate to mention love three times in a letter that emphasizes the unfathomable love of God. This love, faith, grace, and peace all flows from God, the Father of our Lord Jesus Christ.

But notice that Paul adds something here that he has not mentioned in regard to love explicitly (though it has been implied), namely, their love for Christ. He closes with a statement about their personal relationship with Christ. Paul has told them of God's great love, but now we must ask, "Do you love Christ?" Do you love Him? Are you a Christian? Have you turned from sin and placed faith in the Lord Jesus Christ? Do you love Him with an "undying love" that will go on into eternity?

What a great question to end such a letter. Let us love Him! Soon we will see Him, and then we will put our weapons down. Then we will not regret having put all our trust in His perfect work, and we will not regret having been a faithful soldier engaged in his mission.

Colonnaded area in the interior of the Church of St. John at Ephesus.

A CLOSER LOOK

The Sword of the Spirit

I always enjoy visiting places that have old weapons, especially the swords. Sometimes you can see the really big swords in the museums. Some of them weigh more than I do. What many think, as they hold or look on these massive swords, is that they are interesting, but practically useless for modern warfare. No one would recommend them to be issued to troops today. How similar this is to their opinion of the Bible!

Many people admire the Bible, and may put the Bible on display in their home somewhere (normally a huge Bible!); but some of these same people never use the Bible. Why? Like an ancient sword, they deem it useless for their daily battles. It is easy for us to go looking elsewhere for other kinds of weapons in our trials. Have you found yourself doubting that the Bible actually has the power to help you overcome the tactics of the enemy? If so, this should not surprise you. In the garden the Eden, one raised doubt and suspicion about God's Word. But do not be deceived. You can trust God's Word. You need God's Word. Do not go into battle without a sword. Read it. Meditate on it. Pray it. Sing it. Speak it to your brothers and sisters. Proclaim it to the world.

PERSONAL REFLECTION

1. How does Paul summarize many ideas from the previous chapters with this final section on the armor of God?

2. Explain the nature and work of the enemy, based on this passage.

3. Explain the pieces of armor. What does it mean to "take up the armor of God"?

4. Explain how you can use the "sword of the Spirit."

1. John R. W. Stott, *God's New Society: The Message of Ephesians*, The Bible Speaks Today (Downers Grove, IL: InterVarsity Press, 1979), 261.
2. Snodgrass, *Ephesians*. The NIV Application Commentary (Grand Rapids: Zondervan, 1996), 337.
3. Peter T. O'brien, *The Letter to the Ephesians*. The Pillar New Testament Commentary (Grand Rapids: Eerdmans, 1999), 480-81.
4. John Piper, *Let the Nations Be Glad* (Grand Rapids: Baker, 1993), 41.

ABOUT THE AUTHORS

Dr. Tony Merida wrote this personal study guide. Tony is Pastor for Preaching and Vision of Imago Dei Church in Raleigh, N.C. He's also the Dean of Grimké Seminary and Director for Theological Training for Acts 29. Tony has written several books including *The Christ-Centered Expositor* and multiple volumes in the *Christ-Centered Exposition* commentary series. He's happily married to Kimberly, and they have five children.

Kima Jude is a member of The Oaks Baptist Church in Grand Prairie, Texas, where she leads the women's ministry and her husband Barry serves as pastor. Kima has a bachelor's degree in journalism from Marshall University and had an early career as a newspaper reporter followed by a freelance writing career. She has written for several Christian publications, including Lifeway's January Bible Study and several Explore the Bible group plans.

She is employed full-time at a local university in the Dallas-Fort Worth region directing foundation relations and writing proposals. She and her husband are the parents of four young adult children and three young grandchildren. She looks forward to helping them discover the wonder of the Bible.

ALSO AVAILABLE

An item related to teaching this Personal Study Guide is the January Bible Study 2023 Leader Guide (item number: 005837520). The Leader Guide includes commentary, teaching plans, and a redeemable code for a digital download with additional helps.